Heinrich Schenker's theoretical and analytical works claim to resubstantiate the unique artistic presence of the canonic work, and thus reject those musical disciplines such as psychoacoustics and systematic musicology which derive from the natural sciences. In this respect his writing reflects the counter-positivism endemic to the German academic discourse of the first decades of the twentieth century. The rhetoric of this stance, however, conceals a sophisticated program wherein Schenker situates his project in relation to these sciences, arguing his reading of the musical text as a synthesis of a descriptive psychology and an explanatory historiography (which itself embeds both paleographic and philological assumptions). This program is bound up with Schenker's ideological agenda, various aspects of which (the closure of the canon, the filiation of his theory with eighteenth-century predecessors, the dismissal of other theorists and of modern music) are enabled by conceiving this synthesis as a representation of and substitution for the modern musical discourse. This book rereads Schenker's project as an attempt to reconstruct music theory as a discipline against the background of the new empirical musical sciences of the later nineteenth century.

CAMBRIDGE STUDIES IN MUSIC THEORY AND ANALYSIS

GENERAL EDITOR: IAN BENT

SCHENKER'S ARGUMENT AND THE
CLAIMS OF MUSIC THEORY

CAMBRIDGE STUDIES IN MUSIC THEORY AND ANALYSIS

TITLES IN THIS SERIES

SCHENKER'S ARGUMENT AND THE CLAIMS OF MUSIC THEORY

LESLIE DAVID BLASIUS

CAMBRIDGE
UNIVERSITY PRESS

Published by the Press Syndicate of the University of Cambridge
The Pitt Building, Trumpington Street, Cambridge CB2 1RP
40 West 20th Street, New York, NY 10011-4211, USA
10 Stamford Road, Oakleigh, Melbourne 3166, Australia

First published 1996

Printed in Great Britain at the University Press, Cambridge

A catalogue record for this book is available from the British Library

Library of Congress cataloguing in publication data

Blasius, Leslie David, 1955–
Schenker's Argument and the Claims of Music Theory / Leslie David Blasius
p.   cm. – (Cambridge Studies in Music Theory and Analysis)
Includes bibliographical references and index
ISBN 0 521 55085 8 (hardback)
1. Schenkerian analysis. I. Title. II. Series.
MT6.B642S3   1996
781–dc20   95-32682   CIP

ISBN 0 521 55085 8 hardback

AH

CONTENTS

FOREWORD BY IAN BENT

Theory and analysis are in one sense reciprocals: if analysis opens up a musical structure or style to inspection, inventorying its components, identifying its connective forces, providing a description adequate to some live experience, then theory generalizes from such data, predicting what the analyst will find in other cases within a given structural or stylistic orbit, devising systems by which other works – as yet unwritten – might be generated. Conversely, if theory intuits how musical systems operate, then analysis furnishes feedback to such imaginative intuitions, rendering them more insightful. In this sense, they are like two hemispheres that fit together to form a globe (or cerebrum!), functioning deductively as investigation and abstraction, inductively as hypothesis and verification, and in practice forming a chain of alternating activities.

Professionally, on the other hand, "theory" now denotes a whole subdiscipline of the general field of musicology. Analysis often appears to be a subordinate category within the larger activity of theory. After all, there is theory that does not require analysis. Theorists may engage in building systems or formulating strategies for use by composers; and these almost by definition have no use for analysis. Others may conduct experimental research into the sound–materials of music or the cognitive processes of the human mind, to which analysis may be wholly inappropriate. And on the other hand, historians habitually use analysis as a tool for understanding the classes of compositions – repertories, "outputs," "periods," works, versions, sketches, and so forth – that they study. Professionally, then, our ideal image of twin hemispheres is replaced by an intersection: an area that exists in common between two subdisciplines. Seen from this viewpoint, analysis reciprocates in two directions: with certain kinds of theoretical enquiry, and with certain kinds of historical inquiry. In the former case, analysis has tended to be used in rather orthodox modes, in the latter in a more eclectic fashion; but that does not mean that analysis in the service of theory is necessarily more exact, more "scientific," than analysis in the service of history.

The above epistemological excursion is by no means irrelevant to the present series. Cambridge Studies in Music Theory and Analysis is intended to present the work of theorists and of analysts. It has been designed to include "pure" theory – that is, theoretical formulation with a minimum of analytical exemplification; "pure" analysis – that is, practical analysis with a minimum of theoretical underpinning; and writings that fall at points along the spectrum between the two extremes. In these capacities, it aims to illuminate music, as work and as process.

However, theory and analysis are not the exclusive preserves of the present day. As subjects in their own right, they are diachronic. The former is coeval with the very study of music itself, and extends far beyond the confines of Western culture; the latter, defined broadly, has several centuries of past practice. Moreover, they have been dynamic, not static fields throughout their histories. Consequently, studying earlier music through the eyes of its own contemporary theory helps us to escape (when we need to, not that we should make a dogma out if it) from the preconceptions of our own age. Studying earlier analyses does this too, and in a particularly sharply focused way; at the same time it gives us the opportunity to re-evaluate past analytical methods for present purposes, such as is happening currently, for example, with the long-despised methods of hermeneutic analysis of the late nineteenth century. The series thus includes editions and translations of major works of past theory, and also studies in the history of theory.

Schenker's Argument takes as its primary domain the three central "theoretical" texts of that theorist's output: *Harmony* (1906), *Counterpoint* (1910, 1922), and *Free Composition* (1935) – collectively titled his "New Musical Theories and Fantasies" – together with an earlier essay on C. P. E. Bach's ornamentation (1904). Leslie Blasius sets himself the daunting task of placing these four works within their larger intellectual context – or, as he would put it, "situating" them within "the world of musical discourses." In so doing, he reviews the growth of the science of psychology, and advances of the field of philology and economics, in the nineteenth century; also the rise of music criticism in the early nineteenth century, and of textual musicology and of performance practice as would-be sciences in the late nineteenth and early twentieth centuries.

Blasius offers a refreshing exploration of Schenker's theory – or rather, of what made Schenker's theory what it came to be over the thirty years of its inception. He proceeds by a series of investigative moves that thrusts the reader ever deeper into the world of Schenker's thought. Sometimes he pursues false trails (knowingly, I hasten to add) and has to retrace his steps, sometimes he reaches a goal only to find that it provides a temporary or misleading answer, but oftentimes he is rewarded by brilliant insight. On this journey, which has an almost mythic quality to it, he discovers distinctions of which we were unaware, links that we did not suspect, and areas of argument that we never knew existed. The adventure yields numerous surprises and affords some moments of sheer revelation.

In the course of this journey, we come across many different Schenkers: Schenker the historian, Schenker the anti-historian, the editor, the pianist, the performer, the interpreter, the private teacher, the theorist, the ideologue, the canonist, the radical, the conservative . . . Each one we encounter with startling intimacy, as we see them in conjunction with contemporaries such as Edmund Husserl, Wilhelm Dilthey, Hugo Riemann, Guido Adler, and Hans von Bülow, with figures of the past such as Fux, Bach, and Rameau, and tellingly also with figures of the future such as Milton Babbitt, Allen Forte, and Joseph Kerman.

In this book, Blasius has been able to capitalize on the work done by Michel Foucault in constructing an "archeology" of the human sciences. Foucault's enterprise sought to penetrate beneath the world of individual scientists and thinkers, of singular discoveries and specific theories, to a deeper stratum (he called it a "space") at which disciplines that on the surface appear to function very differently can be seen to have profound similarities of behavior ("isomorphisms"), a stratum at which for a particular period the very laws of knowledge themselves operate, and accordingly at which between periods momentous changes take place that range across the face of human knowledge. Blasius's picture of Schenker's world, while in no way derivative, is seen against Foucault's portrayal of the mighty change that occurred between the Classical period and the nineteenth century.

This wonderfully intelligent and clear-thinking book, the thesis of which is presented as a single trajectory to which the footnotes provide an accompanying commentary of almost matching length, enables us for the first time to see the full range of Schenker's thought as a single endeavor.

PREFACE

Among all of the possible theories of music theory, I like to imagine that there is one which might stem from a sociology of the musical discourse (the body of writings in and about music as a whole) and its institutional manifestations. Music theory, within such a sociology, would be defined as a social construction or as a type group behavior rather than as an explanatory mode, and its characteristics explicated in terms of its relations with other group behaviors (such as historical musicology, composition, or musical criticism). Such an investigation might assemble an empirical apparatus of such things as questionnaires, field interviews, and the examination of publication records and hiring and tenure practices, analyze this data in terms of local systems of scales and correlations, and arrive at hypothetical structures of competition and accommodation. Among plausible local studies I can imagine one that attempts to correlate over a specific span of time composers' claims to a theoretical justification for their practice with (let us say) theorists' claims for access to an experiential rather than abstract truth. I can imagine another that examines the institutionalization of different discourses (such as the assignment of a pedagogical priority to music theory and a disciplinary superiority to historical musicology) and the social hierarchies implied by this institutionalization, or a third that reconstructs the ways in which music theory, historical musicology, and music criticism arrive at a division of the corpus of music and the dynamics which underlie this division.

While this hypothetical sociology, were it a reality, might tell us more than we would wish to know, its plausibility points up certain intuitive truths. Music theory (and I use this term loosely, subsuming analysis within theory), almost more than any other strand within the musical discourse, must argue its situation and validity to the world at large. The arguments it makes enable it to gain or retain status at the expense of other studies, to form or break alliances, to construct itself around coherent and unifying methodologies, to create internal hierarchies, and periodically to recenter itself. Some of the strategies it uses to accomplish these tasks are obvious. Music theory (in its analytic practice) can at times lay claim to a vicarious creativity or concreteness denied historical musicology. It constructs specialized vocabularies with which those outside of the theoretical community must come to terms. (Often the success of a theory is indicated by the widespread adoption of its particular technical vocabulary.) It appeals frequently to outside (non-musical) authorities – information theory, psychology, semiotics, phenomenology, cognitive science, feminism, or the like – which stand beyond challenge.

Ultimately, however, the arguments put forward by music theory are uniquely epistemological, deriving from a continuing self-reflection on its own status as musical knowledge, on its grounding in an objective reality. Other domains of the musical discourse are self-reflective. Historical musicology questions its status as an explanatory or critical investigation or questions the place and function of its historiological narratology; and comparative musicology (ethnomusicology) engages in a seemingly endless internal critique of its assumptions, methods, and ideologies. These investigations have at their respective cores, however, a cluster of empirical disciplines – archival research, paleography, textual criticism, field reporting. The particulars of evidence they marshall – the archival entry, the scribal practice, the informant's response – are ultimately and unquestionably factual. Thus, at some level they need never justify their status as knowledge, only the validity of their motivations and interpretations. By contrast, music theory is caught always between the demands that (on the one hand) it report true musical intuitions and (on the other) convince us that these intuitions are real; and even at the most atomic level the "evidence" of theory (be it pitch relations or chords or linear spans) is always constructed rather than factual. Hence music theory finds itself in a state of chronic (if frequently low-level) epistemological crisis. By directly questioning its own basis as a system of knowledge, though, theory can aspire to a priority within the musical discourse, and can claim to examine music before it becomes available to the empirical studies of music.

In fact, we recall quite well that a sophisticated formalism, an attempt to recenter the discourse on unimpeachable epistemological foundations, won for music theory its modern place in the American academy. Admittedly, many of the theorists of the 1960s were concerned with gaining an academic status for musical composition, and thus in a sense coopted music theory as a reflective, pre-compositional activity. This strategy, however, would not have been successful had their theoretical project itself not made radical and striking claims, claims derived from Babbitt's program for an epistemological critique of music theory, its language and suppositions, its structure and internal coherence. The authority of music theory was in fact to derive directly from its self-knowledge, its capacity to (in a sense) be present at its own creation.

It is questionable, though, whether the formalist theorist's bid for an institutional prestige and autonomy would have succeeded without the coincident and charismatic renaissance of the half-century-old music theory of Heinrich Schenker. (This is not to deny that independent "Schenkerian" circles and a more pragmatic middle-group of theorists led by Allen Forte did most of the work of explicating and disseminating Schenker, yet I think it doubtful that Schenker's theory in isolation would have captured such a prominent place in the musical discourse.) This coincidence made for a convenient alliance (if not an alliance of convenience). Schenker's theory, through its analytic practice, made strong claims on musical experience, securing the formalist theorists' flank while they concentrated on theory construction. It held out a complexly ramified explication for the music of the eighteenth and nineteenth centuries, thus implicitly promising an equivalent explication applicable to twentieth-century music. Pragmatically (or politically), it rendered traditional harmonic analysis inadequate or obsolete, thus calling into question an analysis comfortably situated in the methodological heart of music theory's institutional rival, historical musicology.

In two respects, however, this alliance on reflection seems very curious. The first is trivial: Schenker would deny the possibility of further composition, and is indeed strikingly anti-modern in his rhetoric. The second is more striking. The epistemological underpinnings of Schenker's theory are far from obvious. That such underpinnings must exist is evidenced by the claims and demands he makes particularly in his later works: music is to be heard according to the principles he sets out; one must learn and internalize these principles if one is truly to experience the masterwork; some music cannot be experienced in this way (and is therefore, in one sense, not music); other investigations of music must presuppose this experience in order to arrive at a true knowledge. Yet he almost goes out of his way to foreclose any justification for these claims (or his justifications are ideological rather than epistemological).

That Schenker's theory justifies itself by its uncovering of certain musical intuitions is a given. That there is a contradiction between our expectation of some epistemological argument and Schenker's frustration of such is evidenced by a complex of receptions ranging from attempts to represent his theory as a phenomenology or as a sort of proto-generative grammar to attempts to reconstruct his analysis as a formal logic, and by a complex of accommodations or partial readings which take his analysis to be suggestive rather than definitive of a theory of hearing.

The premise of this work, however, is that Schenker has his own epistemology (in the informal sense of the term), one which is masked or displaced from the surface of his texts by ideological manifestos and the like, but which is crucial to the success (both analytic and institutional) enjoyed by his theory. While his rhetoric would seem to foreclose an epistemological reading, it would be unreasonable to assume that the burden of justifying his theory (in a world full of competing music theories, all of which he dismisses) is adequately shouldered only by his ideological postures, and to assume that he does not make some more sophisticated (if implicit) argument for the situation of his text within the world of musical discourses. Indeed, the world of theory is one which would have demanded such an argument. The last quarter of the nineteenth century witnesses a re-creation of the musical discourse in the grand projects of such figures as Helmholtz, Riemann, Wundt, Stumpf, Mocquereau, and Adler. In particular, the study of music gains status within the intellectual world at large through the constitution of two great empirical sciences – the investigation of the psychology of perception (with its foundation in psychoacoustics) and systematic musicology. Figures such as Schering, Wagner, Ludwig, Schoenberg, von Hornbostel, and Kurth in the first quarter of the new century elaborate the work of their predecessors and venture new projects such as comparative musicology (ethnomusicology) and a musical hermeneutics. The place of music theory within this evolving and complex discourse (let alone in its relation to a rapidly evolving compositional practice) is complex and delicate. Theory would seem, in the last quarter of the nineteenth century, the principal beneficiary of the turn to empiricism, recreating itself through a rhetorical alliance with the new musical psychology. Within a generation, however, the contradiction inherent to this alliance, the implausibility of any coherent extrapolation between empirical psychology and music theory comes to the surface, leaving in its wake a theory which both craves the authority of science and yet has abandoned its naive faith in empiricism. Further to unsettle the situation, systematic musicology and the study of musical perception not only constitute themselves as empirical investigations in a way impossible for music theory, but recover or discover musics (and music theories) for which the received doctrines of music theory can provide but scattered and inadequate descriptions. Concomitantly, they undercut the conception of a theory that is simultaneously descriptive and prescriptive. In fact, they would almost create new investigations (such as the comparative study of musical origins, and the reconstruction of music criticism as a hermeneutics) that at some philosophical level compete for music theory's place as a foundational discipline.

It is in this situation that we locate Schenker. In his writings he places his work above or beyond this myriad of new musical sciences and investigations. It is not difficult for us to enumerate reasons for this stance. Given what we can surmise from Schenker's rhetoric about his situation, his sense of rejection, his sense of standing outside the powerful and secure halls of the academy, it is not difficult to see why he feels compelled to claim a kinship with the masters which has been lost by the academicians. (The figures cited above were all successful academics, and all occupied positions of authority. Perhaps significantly, I do not believe that any were Jewish.) Nor should we discount the attractions of a fashionable and general reaction against the positivism of the new musical sciences in the first half of the new century. Yet the very certainty with which Schenker (for whatever reason) dismisses the scientific study of music gives us cause to suspect that at some level his rhetoric conceals a powerful and ramified engagement with the claims of these very investigations that he professes to deny.

As the thesis of this study, therefore, I proceed from the assumption that Schenker's late analysis entails a powerful if unacknowledged epistemological argument, directed first (and most obviously) at the psychologies of music perception available at the opening of the new century, and second (and more importantly) at the sciences of history which flourished simultaneously, and that the strength of his argument is to be found in the combination of these two strands. I assume (as a very schematic historical *a priori*) that we can trace the formation of this argument in his earlier work, and that the evidence of this formation can be extrapolated from those passages which refer (if only obliquely) to investigations which stand outside of music theory, and that this argument is ultimately revealing (in its similarities and differences) of the sort of arguments music theory must assert in order to situate itself within the general musical discourse.

Several points need to be made in regards to this agenda. First, this is a critical rather than explicatory or hermeneutic study. Schenker's theory comes under question in terms of its relations with other investigations rather than as a thing in itself (either as the product of a particular psychology or ideology or as a location in which music is directly addressed). Methodologically, this involves a double bracketing or exclusion, first of the sort of personal or ideological considerations that would be the province of the biographer, and second of the particulars of his theory (scale-steps, unfoldings, the workings of different levels, and the like) that are the province of the music theorist. The Schenker who remains (and comes under examination) is thus an abstract agent within what we might loosely think of as an epistemological economy (i.e. an exchange of arguments as to what constitutes musical knowledge), and the formation of his argument is reconstructed as a series of transactions (overtures, appropriations, rejections) he makes with a field of other investigations.

Second, the fact that this is a critical study determines a somewhat unorthodox style of presentation. Schenker's argument itself is reconstructed (theoretically) within the text. The footnotes and bibliography (beyond their traditional function) constitute a complementary text which locates Schenker's argument within a constellation of other arguments. In other words, at many points the footnotes reconnoiter a discursive terrain which I believe surrounds Schenker's text.

Third, I assume an intertextuality which is not customary to the study of the history of music theory. It would be of intrinsic interest to have a better grasp of what Schenker has read and which figures within the musical discourse at large most occupy him. If Schenker, however, is taken as but one agent within a large epistemological economy (in which every agent is engaged in making some sort of argument), we can assume that there exists a certain body of implicit rules governing the transactions among these agents, that there must be a general consensus about which arguments make sense and which do not, which are effective and which are not. Thus I do not feel it necessary to pursue such normative causal ideas as "influence" or "borrowing" or the like. Rather, I think that in looking (if only quickly) at what sort of work stands alongside that of Schenker, in looking for coincidences, for other arguments, for indications of the respective prestige of other projects, for transactions between other projects, we stand to gain a sense of this body of implicit discursive rules, and a sense of how Schenker uses them to his advantage.

Fourth, I assume that this intertextuality (taken here in the true sense of the word) operates at a different level. I think that the discursive rules that underlie the epistemological economy of music in the latter half of the nineteenth century and the first portion of the twentieth continue to hold to the present. While the substance of the arguments made had to some extent changed, the structure of rules that governs these arguments has not. Were this not the case, I believe that Schenker would today have no more standing than (let us say) Kirnberger or Rameau. On occasion in the first two sections of this text, the footnotes stray outside of the historical bounds of the particular text of Schenker that is under discussion when a path leads interestingly to more recent work. Within the third section of this study, however, I bring Schenker's argument wholly into an engagement with our own discourse about music. This motion hinges on a quick reading of the epistemological archeology of Michel Foucault which I believe provides an insightful map of the epistemological dispositions of the modern human sciences which can be extrapolated to the musical discourse. (This entire work is to some degree informed by Foucault. I make rather more of the psychologism of the later nineteenth century than does he in the first section of my argument, and rather less of the historical consciousness in the second.) Several purposes are served by this move. We gain a purchase on the engagement between Schenker's theory and the epistemologically reflective music theories which came into being in the 1960s, and arrive at a rather different reading of Schenker's appropriation by the modern theoretical community. We also come to see a curious engagement between Schenker's theory and the work of some of the more radical theorists of the later 1970s, and we bring Schenker's analysis into a rather charged encounter with the discipline of music criticism, and ultimately into an encounter with a rather remote critical theory.

Lastly, I would note that the double exclusion which constitutes the methodological premise of this study (the deferral of an explication of his theory and of its hermeneutics) is not absolute. It is impossible to study Schenker's writings from even a very abstract vantage and not arrive at some sort of explication for the particulars of his theory such as strata and prolongation. Nor is it possible to leave his personality and (in particular) his ideology unremarked. Accordingly, the final section of this study brings Schenker's ideology into play, not to explain it, but to demonstrate how his ideological argument operates on his epistemological argument in order to give us the Schenker we know today.

A book (particularly one which has gone through a lengthy gestation) is never completely the product of a single author, and this particular work could not have come into being without the support and contributions of many individuals. Peter Westergaard and Scott Burnham ably critiqued many of the ideas contained herein as they arose in conference papers and my dissertation work. Marjorie Tichenor brought her expertise to bear on my sometimes problematic prose. David Rakowski provided musical examples and (with Beth Wiemann) a place for me to get away from home. Penny Souster, of Cambridge University Press, proved to be an editor both enthusiastic and (fortunately) patient. Ian Bent's contribution has been almost beyond measure: this text would be far poorer without his close attention. Finally, I could not have accomplished this task without the generous encouragement and support of my parents, Gordon and Christina Blasius. To all of these people (and to others too numerous to mention) I give my deepest thanks.

THE APPEAL TO PSYCHOLOGY

A NEW PROGRAM FOR MUSIC THEORY

Schenker moves most decisively in the preface to *Harmony* (1906) to differentiate his work from that of his contemporaries.[1] We are given to understand that his treatise alone is not a low-grade compositional primer but rather a study of the abstract forces underlying music, an investigation of "a purely spiritual universe, a system of ideally moving forces" in which all considerations of voice-leading are to be held in suspension.[2] Thus passages from the masterworks will be correctly interpolated into the text not as exemplary compositional exercises but as phenomenal evidence of the workings of abstract musical laws, and the accustomed division of the harmony treatise into a theory of harmonic analysis and a practice of harmonic voice-leading will give way to a more insightful division between a theory of atemporal tonal systems and a practice of harmonic succession.

1 Heinrich Schenker, *Neue musikalische Theorien und Phantasien*, vol. I: *Harmonielehre* (Stuttgart and Berlin: J. G. Cotta'sche Buchhandlung Nachfolger, 1906); ed. and annotated by Oswald Jonas, trans. Elisabeth Mann Borgese as *Harmony* (Chicago: University of Chicago Press, 1954), xxv–xxvii. All citations hereafter will be to the Borgese translation. Schenker's personality aside, the tone and the claims of this introduction serve a commercial purpose, enabling Schenker's work to compete against an oversupply of "new" harmony treatises appearing in the first decade of the twentieth century. He of course also cites his (fashionable) rejection of the "undertone" series and the symmetric derivation of tonal systems. Among other works which claim radically to correct the field, for example, are Georg Capellen's *Die "musikalische" Akustik als Grundlage der Harmonik und Melodik* (Leipzig: C. F. Kahnt, 1903) and *Die Freiheit oder Unfreiheit der Töne und Intervalle als Kriterium der Stimmführung* (Leipzig: C. F. Kahnt, 1905). (Capellen seems to have been a rising star on the music theory circuit in the first decade of the twentieth century, best known perhaps for his own attack on Riemann's dualist harmony entitled *Die Zukunft der Musiktheorie [Dualismus oder "Monismus"?] und ihre Einwirkung auf die Praxis* [Leipzig, C. F. Kahnt, 1905]. He wrote later on the construction of new notational systems and on "exotic" harmonies.)

2 Schenker, *Harmony*, xxv. The displacement of pragmatic considerations from one text to another has a precedent in Hugo Riemann's complementary *Musikalische Logik: Hauptzüge der physiologischen und psychologischen Begründung unseres Musiksystems* (Leipzig: C. F. Kahnt, 1874) and *Musikalische Syntaxis: Grundriss einer harmonischen Satzbildungslehre* (Leipzig: Breitkopf und Härtel, 1877).

Familiar as we have become with the tenor of Schenker's entire corpus, this program and its realization in the body of *Harmony* may not strike us as radical, and looking even beyond Schenker's own claims, it takes a certain effort for us to recognize that through his abstraction of an essentially conservative harmonic theory he rather spectacularly recuperates two major strands of late nineteenth-century music theory – the pedagogic and the speculative.[3]

Still, one particular usage appearing in both the preface and the body of Schenker's text strikes us as curious. In his consideration of the temporal extension of harmony – the succession of scale-steps – Schenker speaks of the "psychology" of progressions and the "psychology" of chromaticism.[4] This designation might strike us as naive, a sort of passing affectation.[5] More generously, we might see it as simply a concession to an almost automatic turn-of-the-century scientism. Perhaps we should treat it with a certain gravity. The conclusion to the preface of *Harmony* promises a study of the "Psychology of Counterpoint." The first volume of *Counterpoint* (1910) quite logically extends the program of *Harmony* and, accepting the validity of the agenda, most convincingly delivers on this promise of a "psychology

---

3   The distinction between speculative and pedagogic genres extends throughout the history of music theory, reaching back to the medieval separation of texts which draw on the speculative tradition of Boethius and texts which treat the pragmatics of chant. This distinction, though, is frequently elusive, and the engagement between different genres complex. In the eighteenth century, for example, we may speak more accurately of a continuum rather than a division of genres. Rameau's harmonic theory, to take but one instance, both addresses the scientific discourse of his time and attempts to construct a more efficient figured-bass practice. By contrast, in the early nineteenth century the pedagogical tradition (authorized by a humanistic appropriation of the associationist psychology of the eighteenth century) takes on a life of its own. Thus, the harmony primer and the composition handbook are more characteristic of this period than the "scientific" treatise. The persistence of an autonomous pedagogical genre into the early twentieth century is evidenced by Riemann's numerous "catechisms." Schenker, in many places in his writings, severely criticizes this pedagogical genre (which he traces back to Rameau).

4   These chapters are entitled "On the Psychology of Contents and of Step Progression" (*Harmony*, 211) and "On the Psychology of Chromatic Alteration" (*Harmony*, 251).

5   This is the stance taken in Joseph Dubiel's " 'When You are a Beethoven': Kinds of Rules in Schenker's 'Counterpoint' " in the *Journal of Music Theory* 34 (1990), 291–340. Dubiel's review article develops what I might term a genetic explication for Schenker's notion of prolongation, demonstrating how it is logically entailed by the construal of the notion of rules Schenker lays out at the beginning of his study. Dubiel's reading is intricate, insightful, and sympathetic, and locates a convincing reasoning beneath the rhetoric of Schenker's various treatises. His Schenker is more concrete and more balanced than is mine. Much as I admire this reading, however, I think still that we cannot ignore the way in which Schenker's rhetoric is a way of positioning himself within a wider discourse, and thus that we need to give a more serious reading to passages that at first may seem naive or anachronistic.

of counterpoint": through an abstraction of counterpoint in two voices (derived principally from Fux, yet also taking into account the counterpoints of Albrechtsberger, Bellermann, and Cherubini), Schenker claims to systematically catalog the intrinsic affects – the "psychology" – of pitch successions.[6] Accordingly, he takes particular care in decontaminating the *cantus firmus*, purging it of tonal allusion, rhythm, and historicism, claiming that only in a sterile medium can one begin accurately to gauge the specific psychological content of the unfolding of tones. This program gives rise to what is, on first reading, the most striking stance in *Counterpoint* I: Schenker chooses not to forbid arbitrarily contrapuntal motions traditionally held to be faulty, but instead takes pains to demonstrate why such motions are psychologically defective. Finally, we almost need not mention that, as in *Harmony*, Schenker's abstraction allows him to interpolate passages from free composition into the text as evidence of musico-psychological laws discovered in the close examination of counterpoint.

Could it be argued that we make too much of the appeal to psychology in *Counterpoint* I? Schenker himself abandons the term in the second volume of *Counterpoint* (1922).[7] We might do likewise. We cannot but remark, however, that Schenker abandons far more than simply the appeal to psychology in *Counterpoint* II. This second volume of his study presents itself as a straightforward continuation of the first, an extension of the species through three and more voices. As we would expect, Schenker, in

6 Heinrich Schenker, *Neue musikalische Theorien und Phantasien*, vol. II: *Kontrapunkt*, Part 1 (Stuttgart and Berlin: J. G. Cotta'sche Buchhandlung Nachfolger, 1910); ed. and trans. by John Rothgeb and Jürgen Thym as *Counterpoint* (New York: Schirmer Books, 1987), vol. I. All citations hereafter will be to Rothgeb and Thym's translation. In his preface, Schenker filiates his project with the species counterpoint of Fux and the figured-bass method of C. P. E. Bach (which, in reference to my earlier point, returns his theory to a place at which the distinction between the speculative and the pragmatic is not so easily drawn). He points out, however, that Fux conceives counterpoint as vocal composition (and hence that as a method of composition it lacks a future) and that Bach's system has lost a clear grounding in counterpoint. In Schenker's accounting, though, these errors are dwarfed by that of Rameau, who wrongly conflates counterpoint with a primitive scale-step theory (*Counterpoint* I, xxv–xxx). Throughout his counterpoint, Schenker uses Fux, Albrechtsberger, Bellermann, and Cherubini as interlocutors. Their texts, or the (sometimes misconceived) musical intuitions contained in these texts, constitute empirical evidence for the existence of psychological laws. The rationale for theorizing counterpoint (and hence banishing the consideration of such contrapuntal genres as fugue to a future work) is found in Schenker's introduction (*Counterpoint* I, 1–16).

7 Heinrich Schenker, *Neue musikalische Theorien und Phantasien*, vol. II: *Kontrapunkt*, Part 2. (Vienna: Universal Edition, 1922); ed. and trans. by John Rothgeb and Jürgen Thym as *Counterpoint* (New York: Schirmer Books, 1987), vol. II. All citations hereafter will be to Rothgeb and Thym's translation.

the preface to this new study, again claims to redeem the study of counterpoint. Yet here he does not substantiate this claim through the presentation of any explicit program, or (more to the point) re-substantiate it through a recapitulation of the program of *Harmony* or *Counterpoint* I. Rather, the preface to *Counterpoint* II meditates on the decadence of contemporary art and politics, and on the redemptive qualities (both social and musical) of a true understanding of music: indeed, a rather stark ideological rhetoric here replaces the epistemological audacity of its predecessors. Moreover, even the most casual of examinations of the body of *Counterpoint* I demonstrates that that feature which so distinguishes the format of both *Harmony* and *Counterpoint* I, the introduction of passages of free composition in the text as evidence of the laws of musical succession, is absent from this new treatment. (In fact, Schenker rather intriguingly apologizes for his earlier practice of mixing theory and studies of "real music," ascribing this practice to the exigencies of his earlier situation.[8] While he obviously refers to the near simultaneous publication of *Counterpoint* I and his studies of Bach's Chromatic Fantasia and Fugue and Beethoven's Ninth Symphony, we might plausibly, if obliquely, extend this distancing to encompass the interpolation of free composition and theory in *Counterpoint* I.)

What are we to make of these changes? With respect to Schenker's preface, one is almost driven towards some sort of social or biographical explication. While Schenker's biography has yet to be written (perhaps because of his ideological fervor) one certainly is conscious that Schenker's situation after the Great War as an assimilated Jew, a nostalgic monarchist, and a cultural nationalist amidst a deeply traumatized society could not but prompt any manner of striking rhetorical shifts. In fact, current biographical logic would practically demand that one read into the program of *Harmony* and *Counterpoint* I a failed assimilatory strategy.

With regard to the respective bodies of Schenker's texts, our quick turn through *Counterpoint* I and II does not (for narrative reasons) take into account the technical difficulties involved in the appreciation of counterpoint through the addition of voices. As Schenker takes pains to point out, the insertion of an extra voice or voices into the counterpoint constrains the liberty of succession and introduces an element of musical causality reminiscent of free composition; and moreover, the inevitable introduction of *ellipsis* (with the necessity of an implied third voice) brings counterpoint

8   *Counterpoint* II, xii.

to the verge of free composition (with its subsumption of groups of harmonies within the scale-step).[9]

Despite these explications for the disjunction between the world of *Harmony* and *Counterpoint* I and the world of *Counterpoint* II one still returns to the curious notion of a musical psychology and its role in this displacement. We have no evidence as yet with which to make a case for this role. Yet we might put forward an intuition that could well serve as a motivation for constructing just such a case. Assuming this disjunction, one senses, and rather curiously, that the world of *Harmony* and the first volume of *Counterpoint* (in their preoccupation with the underlying laws of music) stands almost closer to the world of Schenker's later analysis (or our received notions of such) than does the world of the second volume of *Counterpoint* (with its hermetic concentration on rules) and that this hypothetical proximity has something to do with Schenker's understanding of psychology. This cannot, of course, be true in a literal sense, yet one suspects that there is some reasoning or some argument to be found in the former pair of works and not in the latter that bears directly on the structure and claims put forward in the analysis with which we are most familiar.

THE PSYCHOLOGISTIC ARGUMENT

We can begin to lay the groundwork for our case by liberating "psychology" from its quotation marks, by revesting the notion of a musical psychology with its full historical context. To extend an earlier intimation, Schenker's evocation of the term "psychology" demands attention not because it is an original move, but rather because within an undeniably original program it is a rather conventional one. Throughout the earlier part of the nineteenth century, the application of the notion of psychology to music can be documented as a convention of what one might call the aesthetic (as opposed to pragmatic) study of music, which (as in Schenker) entails the critical examination of the psychic correlate of internal musical affect.[10] Yet we would do well to recall that by the time of *Harmony* this

---

9 "On the Elision of Voice as Bridge to Free Composition" (*Counterpoint* II, 269–273). Note that this conception of a bridge contradicts the premise of *Counterpoint* I, wherein the error of conflating counterpoint and free composition is seen to be fundamental to the failure of earlier texts.

10 The use of the term "psychology" in musical study can be traced back to the last years of the eighteenth century. The earliest example to which I have found reference is J. J. Rausch, *Psychologische Abhandlung über den Einfluss der Töne, und insbesondre der Musik auf die Seele* (Breslau, 1782) which is cited in Christian Blankenburg's *Litterarische Zusätze zu Johann Georg Sulzers Allgemeine*

conception of psychology as a perhaps intriguing or elegant but certainly vague subsection of natural philosophy has been displaced, that psychology has reinvented itself as an optimistic and prestigious empirical science, and we would also do well to remember that the engagement of this science with the study of music has in the last quarter of the nineteenth century taken on exceedingly rich and strange overtones.[11]

Theorie der schönen Künste, vol. II (Leipzig: Weidmann, 1797; rpt. Frankfurt am Main: Athenäum, 1972), 404. We can conceive the early and middle nineteenth century's psychology of music with most accuracy as an attempt to apply an epistemology of sensation and association (supplemented later by theories of evolutionary function) to the eighteenth century's uncritical assumption that music represents the passions, and thus to conceive a mental calculus of meaning. The two key works of nineteenth-century psychological aesthetics are Eduard Hanslick's *Vom Musikalisch-Schönen* (Leipzig: Rudolph Weigel, 1854) and Herbert Spencer's "The Origin and Function of Music" (1857) in *Essays: Scientific, Political, and Speculative*, vol. I (London: Williams and Norgate, 1868), 210–238. I will at times use the terms "psychologism" or "psychologistic" in preference to "psychology" or "psychological." These terms were first applied to the early nineteenth-century work of Jakob Fries and Friedrich Eduard Beneke, who asserted the philosophical primacy of experience (whose study constitutes psychology) against the transcendentalism of Kant and Hegel (an opposition we might see reflected in that between Hanslick and, let us say, Wagner). In the history of philosophy they have come to apply to any epistemological position which ultimately grounds knowledge in the structure of the mind and presumes that this structure is empirically recoverable.

11 The spectacular opening gambit in the re-empiricization of musical psychology is (of course) Helmholtz's *Die Lehre von den Tonempfindungen, als physiologische Grundlage für die Theorie der Musik* (Brunswick: Friedrich Vieweg, 1862). The work of the first generation of these experimental psychologists – Helmholtz, Fechner, Mach – is properly physiological, allied methodologically with physics, and concerned first with sensation and later with the mechanics of perception. Only in 1879, with the establishment of Wilhelm Wundt's famed laboratory at the University of Leipzig, does one locate an experimental psychology of music which goes beyond the physiological acoustics of Helmholtz, and which with better reason promises an experimental investigation of higher mental functions and a rapprochement with the early speculative tradition of an aesthetic psychology. (In fact, this first generation of experimental psychologists sees their project as the modern successor of traditional philosophy. Wundt, in particular, is a figure of stunning breadth and ambition.) Carl Stumpf, the most famous of Wundt's proteges, regards musical perception in particular as an interesting field of study: see his magisterial *Tonpsychologie*, 2 vols. (Leipzig: S. Hirzel, 1883–1900). The best history of the birth of modern psychology as a methodological and social project is found in Kurt Danziger's *Constructing the Subject: Historical Origins of Psychological Research* (Cambridge: Cambridge University Press, 1990).

Helmholtz sees his study of physical and physiological acoustics as defining an empirically certain ground between the less certain investigations of music theory and psychological aesthetics, particularly that of Hanslick (*Die Lehre*, xxiv). The theorists of the time – Otto Tiersch, Arthur von Oettingen (who held a chair in physics), and Hugo Riemann in particular – could not but see in Helmholtz's work an opportunity to recapture the scientific prestige held by music theory in the eighteenth century. Characteristic of these attempts to recuperate the new acoustics to contemporary theory in the 1870s (specifically, I think, with the theories of Hauptmann) in a single grand system is the notion of a "musical logic." (The enthusiam for the term logic may also derive from the neo-Kantian epistemological renaissance of the last quarter of the nineteenth century.) Riemann's *Musikalische Logik* reconciles Helmholtz's "discovery" of undertones with Oettingen's

Unlike many of his contemporaries, Schenker shows a certain reluctance about being drawn too overtly into the problematic engagement with the empirical study of the sensation and perception of music which had governed much of music theory since the publication of Helmholtz's physiological acoustics. Put with more precision, he is not willing to play to the work of Helmholtz or Mach or Stumpf or Wundt as a verifiably scientific ground for the notion of harmony, nor will he hazard some manner of speculative logic of music which presents itself as a rationalist investigation standing (at least in its own mind) shoulder to shoulder with the muscular investigations of experimental psychology.[12]

We must award Schenker credit for a certain canniness. He coyly avoids the conventional banality of overemphasis of the overtone series as the authorization for triadic harmony, and avoids being drawn into or even engaging such problems of the new psychoacoustics as, for example, the inability to define the perceptual basis for the differentiation of consonance and dissonance – a question that preoccupied the empirical psychologists at the turn of the century.[13] We must assert, however, that while Schenker

symmetrical derivation of major and minor modes. The construction of a musical logic is taken to be the central task of music theory in the disciplinary schema put forward in Guido Adler's "Umfang, Methode und Ziel der Musikwissenschaft" in *Vierteljahrsschrift für Musikwissenschaft* 1 (Leipzig: Breitkopf und Härtel, 1885; rpt. Hildesheim: Georg Olms, 1966), 5–20.

12 I would point out, though, that much of the naive enthusiam for the psychologistic agenda seems to have foundered by the turn of the century. A faith in the ultimate explanatory power of psychology is still to be found, and the low-level appeal to the overtone series as a justification for tonal harmony remains a staple of the theory treatise. Georg Capellen, in *Die "musikalische" Akustik*, gives a series of "experiments" involving simultaneously silent and struck keys to demonstrate this point: Schenker knows this work, and refers to it negatively (*Counterpoint* I, 193). A later take on his conception of the relation of psychology and music is found in an article reviewing the theory found in Robert Mayrhofer's *Psychologie des Klanges und die daraus hervorgehende theoretisch-praktische Harmonielehre nebst den Grundlagen der klanglichen Ästhetik* (Leipzig: Schuberth, 1907) and *Die organische Harmonielehre* (Berlin and Leipzig: Schuster & Loeffler, 1908) entitled "Robert Mayrhofers Organische Harmonielehre und die moderne Theorie" in *Die Musik* 9/6 (December, 1909) 346–357. But it is interesting that Riemann himself feels compelled maturely to reassess (and reassert) the relation between the psychology of music and the theory of music in his "Ideen zu einer 'Lehre von den Tonvorstellungen'" in *Jahrbuch der Musikbibliothek Peters für 1914/1915*. 21/22 (1916; rpt. Vaduz: Kraus, 1965) 1–26; introduced and translated by Robert Wason and Elizabeth Marvin as "Riemann's 'Ideen zu einer "Lehre von den Tonvorstellungen"': an Annotated Translation" in the *Journal of Music Theory* 36 (1992) 69–117; and his "Neue Beiträge zu einer Lehre von den Tonvorstellungen" in *Jahrbuch der Musikbibliothek Peters für 1916*. 23 (1917; rpt. Vaduz: Kraus, 1965), 1–21. Needless to say, some theorists did still remain enthusiastic: the apogee of the psychological harmony is found in Sigfrid Karg-Elert, *Die Grundlagen der Musiktheorie*, Part II: *Harmonielehre* (2nd edn. Leipzig: Speka-Musikalienverlag, 1921).

13 The phenomenon of consonance, easily defined within the framework of eighteenth-century whole-number acoustics in terms of the first six whole-number ratios, becomes quite problematic

plays down any immediate appeal to some "natural science" of music, he does without question smuggle the notion of a natural science of music into *Harmony* and (particularly) into the first volume of *Counterpoint* in the form of a fairly sophisticated psychological argument.

One speaks not of the rather obvious appeal earlier rehearsed, but of evidence more subtle. Rhetorically, this covert appeal to natural science is evidenced in the quotation from *Harmony's* preface which opened the chapter: regardless of Schenker's positing of a "purely spiritual universe," his evocation of a "system of ideally moving forces" clearly refers to the conceptions of physics, the paradigmatic discipline for all of the natural sciences in the nineteenth century. Conceptually, we note that the first volume of *Counterpoint* (which embodies the influence of natural science more directly than *Harmony*) presents counterpoint as almost a cultural psychology wherein the psychological laws of music are revealed through close scrutiny of the accumulated (if unexamined) insights of centuries of Western musicians as evidenced in the work of Schenker's predecessors (Fux, Cherubini, Bellermann, Albrechtsberger, *et al.*)[14]

in the nineteenth century on the realization that tones themselves are complex rather than simple events. Helmholtz accounts for the discrimination between consonance and dissonance through the acoustic phenomenon of beating. Stumpf postulates a mental mechanism of "fusion." Competing theories account for this discrimination by hypothesizing about the mutual reinforcement of summation and difference tones (Krueger), or the subconcious gauging of micro-rhythms (Lipps). Wundt, with more sophistication, notes that the distinction between consonance and dissonance is contextual, and hypothesizes that the perception of this distinction is actually a complex of several perceptual mechanisms. A tendentious but interesting and contemporary discussion of these respective theories is found in Theodor Lipps, *Psychological Studies,* trans. Herbert Sanborn (Baltimore: Williams and Wilkins, 1926), 138–265. A modern survey is found in Albert Wellek, *Musikpsychologie und Musikästhetik; Grundriss der systematischen Musikwissenschaft* (Frankfurt am Main: Akademische Verlagsgesellschaft, 1963). Interestingly enough, Schoenberg picks up on this problem, arguing that the failure to define consonance and dissonance is sufficient reason to hold this distinction under suspicion. See his *Theory of Harmony*, trans. Roy Carter (Berkeley: University of California Press, 1978), 18–22.

14 This line of thought is a stretch, yet Schenker's turn to a conventional psychology is so remarkable in context as to justify some speculation. The notion of a cultural psychology (a "Völkerpsychologie") may be credited to Wundt, who feels that certain portions of the human psychology (memory and thought) are unavailable to conventional experimental procedures and thus can be extrapolated only through the examination of cultural artifacts (behaviors and the like), particularly those of more "natural" or uncontaminated societies. See his *Probleme der Völkerpsychologie* (Leipzig: E. Wiegandt, 1911). Musically important works in this area include Richard Wallaschek's *Anfänge der Tonkunst* (Leipzig: J. A. Barth, 1903), which is particularly interesting in assigning priority to the "time-sense" of music, and Stumpf's *Die Anfänge der Musik* (Leipzig: J. A. Barth, 1911). Adler assigns this discipline an independent (if subordinate) position in his schema, and in a very real way this inquiry, in the first decade of the century, displaces music theory as a disciplinary complement of physiological and psychological acoustics. This is the domain from which arises the discipline of

Even more subtly, we can look to Schenker's reaffirmation of the organization of counterpoint by species. While we are tempted to read this move as Schenker presents it, as a traditionalist rejection of "modern" stylistic counterpoint, we remind ourselves that it is also the means for abstracting counterpoint from composition. By contrast or extension we can recognize that the systematic development of contrapuntal motions through the species is itself a scientific strategy, that while for Schenker the science of the species does not (as it does for Fux) lie in the classification of various musical moments according to an underlying taxonomy, the system of species recreates (as a didactic situation) the experimental procedure of natural science, that counterpoint comes in all respects to replicate the scientist's laboratory (or at least its pedagogical counterpart).

Granted, though, the argument for a systemic and even sophisticated psychologism in the first volume of *Counterpoint* (or for that matter in *Harmony*), we cannot ignore the obvious limits to this psychologism. Perhaps the only valid empiricism of Schenker's investigation lies in the close reading of Fux, Cherubini, and company, and even here, he injects his own opinions and evaluations with such frequency as to undercut rhetorically any pretense of objectivity. Moreover, except in the restricted sense that the creation of *cantus firmi* and their accompanied contrapuntal lines could be said to be open-ended, Schenker's take on counterpoint would seem to be rather easily exhausted. It is far from likely that the consideration of additional counterpoint treatises in the manner of *Counterpoint I* would have yielded Schenker a more insightful or scientific result.

Thus, even if we choose not to read the abandonment of the rhetoric of psychological "laws" in *Counterpoint* II as the result of a biographical or ideological shift, we are led alternatively to read this abandonment as the product of an inevitable recognition on the part of Schenker of the inherent limits of his earlier incorporation of natural science.

comparative musicology (or by the modern usage, ethnomusicology): the work of Abraham and von Hornbostel appears first in Stumpf's *Beiträge zur Akustik und Musikwissenschaft*, 9 vols. (Leipzig: J. A. Barth, 1898–1924). It also, however, gives rise to a continuing study of folksong. For example see Albert Wellek, *Typologie der Musikbegabung im deutschen Volke; Grundlegung einer psychologischen Theorie der Musik und Musikgeschichte* (Munich: C. H. Beck, 1939). Schenker is disparaging of folk music in general, and the study of "folk-tonality" in particular: his one citation of Helmholtz attacks the latter's rejection of the western harmonization of non-western music (*Counterpoint* I, 29). One suspects that given his notion of "artistic selection" he would disapprove of comparative musicology in general. Yet it remains that he appropriates for his own purpose the theoretic move of the cultural psychologists, looking to a simpler music in order to gain a psychological insight.

Perhaps, though, we all to easily settle for the obvious reading once again when we can salvage our line of inquiry by bringing to life the context within which Schenker is writing. The case for a psychologistic turn-of-the-century Schenker is plausible only when the prestige of the psychological sciences of the time and the impressive intellectual standing of such figures as Stumpf and Wundt (and the expectations of the theoretical community) are taken into consideration. Although we know Schenker to be writing in a place somewhere beyond the intellectual and social boundaries of German academe, we would err in isolating him from the powerful events reshaping German intellectual society (even if we do only read him as a strong if undeniably conservative thinker who resists being drawn too closely into the orbit of the pervasive psychologism of the time). In fact, we might profitably conceive a Schenker who is more deeply sensitive to the epistemological undercurrents of the academy.

To substantiate this hypothesis, we need to take into account a crisis within the psychological paradigm and a powerful counter-psychologistic argument (one which at least questions the nature if not the necessity of psychologism) which takes shape at approximately the same time as Schenker's earlier writings. We can locate with precision the germ of this critique of psychologism in a justly notorious essay written by the humanist Dilthey and entitled "Ideas Concerning a Descriptive and Analytic Psychology" (1905).[15] Dilthey diagnoses an epistemological dilemma in the human sciences of his time in which these sciences are forced to choose between the naive appeal to some manner of scientific psychology and an anti-interpretive positivism. (By "human sciences," he refers explicitly to historiography and the studies of the respective foundations of law and religion, yet by inference he seemingly includes the studies of art and aesthetics and, adjacently, the study of epistemology.) He concedes

15 Wilhelm Dilthey, "Ideen über eine beschreibende und zergliedernde Psychologie" *Gesammelte Schriften* V (Stuttgart: Teuber, 1957), 139–240; trans. Richard Zaner as "Ideas Concerning a Descriptive and Analytic Psychology" in *Descriptive Psychology and Historical Understanding* (The Hague: Martinus Nijhoff, 1977). Dilthey is without doubt the central figure in the study of the human sciences in the later nineteenth century (the notion of "human sciences" is his), involved particularly in the reconstruction of a historical and cultural hermeneutics. His distinction between the *Geisteswissenschaft* and the *Naturwissenschaft* plays an increasingly important role in early twentieth-century German intellectual thinking, and still has a resonance today. Although I would not make the claim that anything to be found in Schenker derives directly from Dilthey, it is implausible that any figure of the time with a reasonable education would have been unaware of Dilthey (any more than a comparable figure in the last decade would have been unaware of Derrida), and it would have been impossible not to be indirectly familiar with the intellectual currents he set in motion.

the necessity for a strong understanding of psychology as the underpinning for his projected hermeneutics of the human sciences. He does not, however, concede the adequacy of the empirical psychologies of his contemporaries to this task. This assertion is itself unremarkable, as the contemporary psychologists thought of their science as still in its infancy. Dilthey, though, makes an insightful leap. He conceives the problem as not one of extension but rather one of intention. He asserts that the epistemological inadequacy of contemporary psychology stems not from any poverty of accomplishment but rather from a habitual accommodation to the world view of the natural sciences, an automatic equation of psychic phenomena and natural phenomena. In addressing the psychologies of the nineteenth century (not simply the experimental psychologies of the later nineteenth century but also the systems of Herbart, Spencer, Mill, and the associationists), he finds them flawed (at least from the standpoint of the human sciences) in so far as they are grounded locally in the formulation of hypotheses that attempt to locate causal relations between underlying psychic mechanisms and psychic phenomena and globally in the assumption that consciousness is the product of the interaction of these elementary psychic mechanisms. How, he asks, are psychic causalities to be verified beyond the most local of levels? How can any more powerful chemistries of elementary psychic functions move beyond the domain of the hypothetical?

At this juncture, we may have some reservations about the relevance of Dilthey's rather elevated critique to the pragmatics of Schenker's theory (although the reservations we have located in *Harmony* and *Counterpoint* I perhaps reflect less a personal and more a general unease with the claims made for psychology). Dilthey's solution to the problem of an epistemic psychology is, however, powerfully suggestive. He decides that what is needed to set the psychological grounding of the human sciences on track, to find a substantive mediation between the acceptance of a naturalistic psychology and the utter rejection of psychologism, is a new sort of critical psychology, one which unlike its predecessors is not explanatory and constructivist but descriptive and analytic. Specifically, he proposes an investigative agenda that abandons the search for local causation and the attempt to assemble a picture of psychic life as a compound of these causalities in favor of a carefully gauged inferential and introspective examination of the nexus of lived experience as a whole, an analysis of the functional structure of this nexus (Dilthey begins to map this structure in terms of superimposed systems of sensation and perception, feeling and instinct, and volition) and of its development whose result will be a description of consciousness that can serve for the human sciences a function analogous to that provided by mathematics for the natural sciences.[16]

This prescription is as vague as it is ambitious. Dilthey himself makes only tepid claims that the elaboration of such a descriptive and analytic psychology could ever approach completeness or certainty (and thus ever take on its projected function). His own work favors a flexible and intuitive hermeneutics, and there is little evidence of any such psychology being put forward by other authors as the grounds for the study of social artifacts.

While Dilthey's psychology never moves from the domain of the hypothetical to the domain of the actual, his critique as a whole has radical and demonstrable consequences in line with its notoriety. It quite overtly supports Dilthey's own distinction between *Naturwissenschaft* and *Geisteswissenschaft*, a distinction which energizes both late-Imperial and Weimar intellectual debate.[17] Beyond this, we would point out that Husserl

16 Dilthey's championship of an introspective methodology is in itself not remarkable (the notion of introspection being raised as early as the psychologistic epistemologies of Fries and Beneke). The rigorous reporting of subjective experience comes to displace the quantitative measure of an experimental subject's reactions as the methodological protocol of Wundt's laboratory (see Danziger, *Constructing the Subject*, 18–24). In fact, Wundt's students held the strictly quantitative procedures of such predecessors as Helmholtz to be hopelessly old-fashioned. Wundt himself supplies the intellectual framework for this investigation by speaking of the structure of consciousness, specifically proposing that systems of sensation and feeling can be isolated and examined through introspection. (The system of volition, by contrast, is to be studied through his anthropological psychology.) Thus, Dilthey's program is revolutionary not in its championship of introspection, nor in its postulation of a structure of consciousness, but in its rejection of the notion of isolated mental events which can be specifically targeted within carefully drawn "experiments." For a good overview of Wundt's system, and his very impressive epistemology, see Willem van Hoorn and Thom Verhave, "Wilhelm Wundt's Conception of the Multiple Foundations of Scientific Psychology" in *Wilhelm Wundt, progressives Erbe, Wissenschaftsentwicklung und Gegenwart: Protokoll des internationalen Symposiums, Leipzig, 1. und 2. November 1979* (Leipzig: Karl-Marx-Universität, 1980), 107–120.

17 The outstanding history of this period is Pamela Maxine Potter, Trends in German Musicology, 1918–1945: The Effects of Methodological, Ideological, and Institutional Change on the Writing of Music History (Ph.D. dissertation, Yale University, 1991). For a discussion of this controversy see pp. 1–17. Potter's work brings alive the notion of a sociology of the musical discourse, of different methodologies or epistemologies competing for institutional prestige and rewards. With regard to this work, she details the almost visceral reaction against positivism in the post-war period, thus providing another framework within which to regard Schenker's own rejection of "science." (Needless to say, I think that his rejection is rather more complex than would seem apparent at first.) She is also very good on the various strains of German nationalism which infected most of the musicologists of the period. Her tale, when all is said and done, is very sobering, and more than a few of the figures cited in this text are incriminated by their actions between the wars. Her work should perhaps be required reading for all musicologists and theorists.

acknowledges the debt owed by his phenomenological psychology (which he began to work on in 1905) to Dilthey's essay, that we can glimpse Dilthey's prescription at work in his own field of historiography in Collingwood's theory of re-enactment, that empirical psychology itself undergoes a radical methodological extension at about this time which seems to incorporate more than a few of Dilthey's ideas, and that we might reach so far as to see in Freud's clinical analysis of the psyche a reconciliation between descriptive and explanatory psychologies.[18]

Thus, while we would shrink from presenting Dilthey's essay as an active agent in Schenker's thinking, it is not out of the bounds of conjecture to extend our reading of a psychologistic Schenker through his post-*Counterpoint* I evolution in terms of a general motion derived ultimately from Dilthey's agenda. Dilthey envisions an autonomous and universal psychology that could be applied to the human sciences, while Schenker could, at most, be said to posit a heuristic psychology particular to music. We need, though, no coincidence of program to draw on Dilthey in articulating a kindred (if unarticulated or suppressed) auto-critique on the part of the later Schenker, one which motivates a turn from the conceit of the laboratory (with its simple notion of musical causality) toward a more powerful description of musical experience.

THE CONTRAPUNTAL LABORATORY

To reconstruct such an auto-critique in Schenker's evolution, we need first to arrive at a more complex description of the psychologism in

18 For Husserl's account of this motion, and the contribution of Dilthey, see his *Phänomenologische Psychologie. Vorlesungen Sommersemester 1925*, translated by John Scanlon as *Phenomenal Psychology* (The Hague: Martinus Nijhoff, 1977), 1–37. Early on, R. G. Collingwood rejects empirical psychology and the model of natural science as the basis for any historiographical practice. The best summation of his ideas from this period is to be found in his discussion of historiography in *Speculum Mentis: or, The Map of Knowledge* (Oxford: Clarendon Press, 1924), 201–246. Between 1903 and 1913, a program called systematic experimental introspection is the dominant methodology in psychological circles. (This is sometimes referred to as the school of structural psychology.) In extending the introspective methodology to encompass areas Wundt had ruled beyond its reach, areas such as memory, thoughts, and volition (this is the school which holds to the concept of a mental image), the systematic introspectionists might be seen to counter Dilthey's program by emulation. Wundt himself turns his attention to the grounding of the human sciences in his late *Logik*, vol. III: *Logik der Geisteswissenschaften*. (Stuttgart: F. Enke, 1883; 2nd edn. 1908). Regardless, it is the sudden collapse of this movement which shifts the focus of psychological investigation from consciousness and experience either to the unconscious or to function and behavior, and which leads to a final divorce of psychology from philosophy. Freud's views regarding the situation of his

Example 1
(a) Beethoven, Op. 53, I. mm. 34–39
(b) Chopin, Op. 30, No. 4, mm. 128–32

Counterpoint I. To accomplish this, we turn to the area in *Counterpoint* I wherein Schenker addresses the similar motion of (and motion to) perfect consonances in the first species.[19] In general terms, Schenker (within this discussion) first enumerates the psychological factors underlying such motions (the nature of perfect consonances, the general character of similar motion, the "meaning" of polyphony as the manifestation of autonomous voices) and then argues the prohibition of parallel octaves and unisons and the problematic nature of similar motion to these intervals in the counterpoint (and hence their particular affect in free composition) from the general contrapuntal prohibition of repetition and from the need to keep two voices distinct.

One passage within this section – an extended digression, in fact – is particularly teasing in so much as Schenker devotes a great deal of work to a seemingly minor point.[20] He takes pains to distinguish between octave and fifth parallels, particularly to disabuse the reader of any notion that like the octave, the fifth can be considered at times a doubling. He first traces the prohibition of parallel fifths from the constitution of the fifth as harmonic norm in the practice of organum (the product of misguided or misapplied theorizing) through the introduction of imperfect consonances into organum and to a consequent instinctual realization of the suitability of imperfect consonance (and unsuitability of the fifth) to parallel motion (a practice codified in the theories of Johannes de Muris). He then introduces two passages from free composition, the opening of the second theme of the first movement of Beethoven's Piano Sonata Op. 53 and a closing passage from Chopin's Mazurka Op. 10, No. 4 (Ex. 1a,b), pointing out how they respectively incorporate disjunct and conjunct parallel fifths, and proceeding to explain that in neither case can the fifth be considered a doubling.[21] At this point, however, his argument takes an unexpected turn. Rather than unpacking his assertion (an explication he promises for later), he turns to the literature on fifth successions. Hauptmann's distinction between parallel fifth and octave successions gains Schenker's approbation (although the reasoning of Hauptmann's argument merits a swift condemnation). Riemann's thinking on the matter, which Schenker himself feels

psychoanalysis in relation to experimental and descriptive psychologies are to be found in the opening of his *Introductory Lectures on Psychoanalysis*, trans. James Strachey (New York: W.W. Norton, 1966), 20–21.
19 *Counterpoint* I, 131–132.
20 *Counterpoint* I, 132–134.
21 *Counterpoint* I, 133–140.

he must present in part in Riemann's own words before rehearsing the remainder of the argument, is another matter. The quotation reads:

A voice that repeatedly presents the octave-tones of the other voice is only a reinforcement of the sound of that second voice; it is not a different voice. And a voice that moves in *parallel fifths* [Schenker's emphasis] or twelfths with a second voice *also* fuses much too completely with the latter to be regarded as an independent voice.[22]

To paraphrase the remainder of the argument, the prohibition of both consecutive fifths and octaves in counterpoint derives from their inherent fusion of two pitches. In fact, Riemann proposes a scale ranging from the strong fusion of the octave through the middling and weak fusions of the fifth and third. Although consecutive octaves and fifths occur in free composition, particularly in orchestral music, the student is to be cautioned against such motions until she or he is able to distinguish parallels which serve as reinforcements (which are allowed in modern practice, particularly when compensated for by contrary motion or dissonance) from parallels between real voices (wherein the parallel fifth is always a stylistic error). Schenker finds fault with each of these points. He directs the reader's attention to the undefined or shifting grounds on which Riemann founds his prohibition. If, for Riemann, there is a continuum of musical artifacts on which are arrayed everything from school exercises in two-voice counterpoint or harmonic voice-leading to examples of free composition as varied as full-textured keyboard works and orchestral pieces, at what point on this continuum does the absolute prohibition against the perfect parallel motion lose its status? Why does it lose its status? What, in free composition, constitutes a "reinforcement" and what constitutes a prohibited parallel within "real voices"?

In working through these objections we glimpse a sort of reasoning in *Counterpoint I* previously unsuspected. Schenker's critique, up to this point, is overtly methodological. Riemann's theory fails as a result of its inability to define a stable and circumscribed body of evidence. It is not simply inconsistent (the prohibition of parallel perfect intervals standing as a stylistic law, yet a law which does not apply equally in all situations) but contrafactual. Not only do consecutive fifths and consecutive octaves make

---

22 Quoted in *Counterpoint* I, 135, 353: Rothgeb and Thym attribute the quotation to Riemann's *Handbuch der Harmonielehre* (Leipzig: Breitkopf und Härtel, 1887; 3rd edn., 1898), 29ff. I have found this quotation in the 5th edition of the same work on p. 34. I have translated *Verschmelzungen* as "fusion" rather than Rothgeb and Thym's "blending."

for distinct affects, they are never (by Riemann's own admission) handled the same way in free composition, yet Riemann does not distinguish between the two situations.

Schenker seems most vexed, however, by Riemann's conflation of octaves and fifths (this being the theme of the digression) and the remainder of his critique turns on this point. Riemann speaks of both octaves and fifths as "reinforcements." While one can easily accept the notion of octave "reinforcement," does not Riemann himself rule out fifth doubling (though, significantly, not octave doubling) of some "real voice"? By what logic is one to identify one tone a fifth above another with the third partial of the first tone, particularly as each unfolds its own unique system of partials? Why is Riemann's notion of reinforcement confined to the second through the fourth partials? Why does it not extend to the ninth or fifteenth partials?

In this last series of questions we hear Schenker's voice rather differently. Schenker now sees Riemann's methodological failure compounded by what we cannot but term an explanatory failure. He quite accurately reads Riemann's evocation of "fusion" as an appeal to some manner of musical-psychological mechanism, and in fact, we know that Riemann appropriates this term from the empirical investigations of the phenomena of consonance as a mental phenomenon in Herbart, Wundt, and Stumpf.[23] What bothers Schenker is not the stragegy of appealing to a psychological mechanism, but rather the mechanism of fusion itself. Quite simply, he states that while the proposition of a graded tonal fusion is "attractive in itself," it conflicts with the evidence of the ear, and hence is contrafactual.

Thus, when he comes at last to pay off on his original promise to explain why the fifth, unlike the octave, can never constitute a doubling, this explanation must unfold not simply against the context of Riemann's "enlightened" recourse to the notion of fusion but against the musical-

---

23 The notion of "fusion" plays a prominent role throughout the discourse of nineteenth-century psychology, so much so as to sensitize us to any incidental usage. Herbart's psychology defines fusion as one of the two ways in which concepts combine to form a greater whole, fusion being the incomplete or reseparable mixture of concepts. Stumpf initially explains the phenomenon of consonance through a developed notion of fusion (although he later abandons it for the notion of "concordance"). Riemann draws on Stumpf's theory, although he points out its drawbacks. Stumpf repays the compliment: he declares harmonic dualism a fiction. See Riemann, *Grundriss der Musikwissenschaft*, 4th edn., ed. Johannes Wolf (Leipzig: Quelle & Meyer, 1928), 53. This work contains also an invaluable bibliography. See Stumpf, "Konsonanz und Konkordanz" in the *Beiträge zur Akustik und Musikwissenschaft* 6 (Leipzig: J. A. Barth, 1911), 116–150. It is perhaps of interest that fusion is taken as one of the principal mechanisms of psychopathology in Freud's theory.

psychological discourse as a whole. To expand this point, Schenker's initial conceit in *Counterpoint* I is, as previously noted, to set counterpoint (figuratively) in the laboratory, to define and gauge empirically the intrinsic affect of tonal combinations. In order to gain some sort of consistency (or pedagogical efficacy) for this laboratory, *Counterpoint* I incorporates a certain amount of explication. Schenker's reading of Riemann gives us to realize that this domain of explanation is more important than we might have thought, that his entire work is underpinned by an engagement with the method of empirical psychology. Following Schenker, the affectual distinction between octaves and fifths becomes obvious when conceiving them as doublings of a line. This distinction cannot but arise from a distinction between two hypothetical psychic operations: the fifth cannot double a line in the same manner as can the octave because while the octave is perceived as an identity, the fifth is perceived as a boundary.[24] (When the first six partials which define the triad are collapsed to a single octave, the third and sixth partials define the outer boundary of the complex.) This explanation is itself situated within a more general hypothesis of interval perception which, in addition to the operations of "identity" and "bounding," includes the operation of "inversion." The third, for example, occupies its peculiar place in counterpoint because it is the single primary consonance which does not call forth any of these mental operations.[25] The fourth is prohibited as a simultaneity (though accepted as a succession) in two-voice counterpoint because it is a second-order "bounding" interval: it is heard as the inversion of a bounding fifth, thus demanding a space of succession to be perceived (or perhaps, we might say, apperceived).[26] By contrast, while the perception of the sixth involves the operation of inversion, it does not involve the operation of bounding, requiring less in the way of mental work, hence leaving the sixth available for use as a simultaneity.[27]

While this complex of hypothetical operations concerning interval perception suggests an unexpected turn in Schenker's thinking, placing it in surprising proximity to empirical investigation of the subject (the study of harmonic intervals being the most highly developed problem in contemporary psychology), it is not the only such complex. Surely

---

24 Schenker has of course previously explicated the content of the fifth in his discussion of the cantus firmus. (Part I, Chap. 2, §12, p. 79).

25 *Counterpoint* I, Part I, Chap. 2, §14, p. 81.

26 *Counterpoint* I, Part I, Chap. 2, §13, pp. 79–81 and (in an extended discussion) Part II, Chap. 1, §3, pp. 112–124.

27 *Counterpoint* I, Part I, Chap. 2, §15, pp. 81–83; and Part II, Chap. 1, §4, pp. 124–126.

Schenker's harmonic theory (at one level) and his contrapuntal theory (at another) both suppose a "grouping" operation (although grouping would most probably have to be taken as itself a complex of primitive operations). Indeed, the most striking feature of *Harmony* is its sophisticated treatment of grouping. Likewise, both suppose an "unpacking" operation wherein certain events are heard as condensations of classes of events. In one instance, Schenker seems to posit a "scaling" operation in which an event isolable within the counterpoint is dimensionally altered in free composition, asserting, more specifically, that the stepwise passing motion filling a third in second species counterpoint (which is, in so far as the passing note resists being grouped with either preceding or succeeding consonance, the sole dissonance allowed in second species) is "scaled-up" in free composition when a fourth is filled by a step and leap.[28]

Granted, one might (justifiably) object that such "operations" are only sporadically encountered in *Counterpoint* I and that they serve not an epistemological but a rhetorical purpose (constituting a convenient means for transferring the authority behind contrapuntal prescriptions from the author to a general and impersonal science). But if we assume that Schenker puts forward these operations in good faith (even if to our minds there is something suspect in this mode of explication) we are given a picture of Schenker's treatise in which an underlying stratum of operations serves an important function (which shall be detailed as follows).

As we have established, Schenker's counterpoint is rationalized as a laboratory within which (in principle) the reader is sensitized to the unique psychological loading of particular pitch combinations. This presentation

---

28 *Counterpoint* I, 184–189. This discussion is to be found in the section entitled "The psychological significance of the passing dissonance" (Part II, Chap. 2, §6). Certainly this discussion of the passing tone is in accord with his later canonic definition of the composing-out of the consonance. However, we should note that he has earlier attempted to treat the psychological content of the second in isolation (§16, pp. 83–84). It is his failure to define a perceptual mechanism (or combination of mechanisms) underlying the second that opens the notion of psychological content as a function: he speculates at the end of his discussion of the second that it may function within the tonal system as a means of gauging the larger intervals. Thus the "scaling" of the second in free composition is logically entailed by its earlier treatment as a function rather than as a complex of operationally-determined qualities. (Schenker does in his first discussion of the second speak of it as the fifth of a fifth, and thus lacking an immediate rapport with the fundamental of an implicit triad. In terms of a calculus of psychological operations, the second might therefore be defined as a complex of two bounding and one inversional operations. Perhaps, if Schenker had been willing to pursue this mode of psychological explication, he would have arrived at the notion of the two bounding operations cancelling each other (or something of the kind) and thus rendering the second "unhearable" outside of a context.

carries with it a particular danger, however, if only implicitly. It suggests that music can be read as a system of discrete and stable affects. It potentially represents musical succession as an *ars combinatoria* of fixed and commensurable psychological atoms (embedded, of course, in an atemporal musical space fixed by scale and mode). When pursued to its logical conclusion, this representation could almost give rise to an analytic meta-language that would, through some sequence of symbols, express the psychological content of passages or pieces. (Taken trivially, Schenker's harmony might be said to constitute just such an analysis, though one might imagine some analytic notation derived from figured bass notation annotated and ligated to reflect harmonic groupings – a sort of contrapuntally aware counterpart to Riemann's analytic reduction to a harmonically annotated and grouped melody line.)[29]

The hazards of just such an analytic methodology are immediately apparent. We would expect Schenker, beyond all other theorists, to be wary of just such an analytic reduction, and indeed, he makes a number of significant moves to foreclose this possibility. Regardless of his stated program, he scrupulously confines encounters between theory and free composition in *Harmony* and *Counterpoint* I to single affects and brief passages composed of single affects. Only on a single occasion in *Counterpoint* I, and then only as an aside, does he read a passage as a sequence of discrete affects.[30] More importantly, he forecloses affective reduction by broadening his theoretical agenda to encompass the deeper strata of explanation and operations, by defining affect as something not functionally irreducible but rather the product of the complex interactions of

29 A simple system of psychoacoustic reading marks figures into Capellen's discussion of melody in his *Fortschrittliche Harmonie- und Melodielehre* (Leipzig, C. F. Kahnt, 1908), 20–22. Riemann thinks of his own analytic shorthand, wherein a condensed melodic line is annotated by phrase groupings, reading marks, and harmonic indication as such a psychological or experiential record. We should not, however, confine our imaginations to such simple analyses. An analysis might very well evolve its own system of symbols. In fact, one can imagine a more radical analysis which bypasses given theoretic notions such as harmony and which, through some rigorous introspective protocol (such as those devised by the experimentalists) attempts qualitatively to capture the experiential substance of each individual musical event. One might also imagine an analytic system which arises from the notion of mental operations, perhaps one which (in line with Schenker's notions of perceptual timing) assumes differing spaces of perception for differing combinations of intervals. For example, a simple closed-position triad might be assumed to take up less of a mental space than a closed-position triad in the first inversion (which contains the complex interval of the fourth), and an analytical system reflecting this distinction might be devised, one perhaps assigning different sizes of noteheads according to degree of complexity. Such a symbol system would not necessarily have been an anomaly in Schenker's time, and today would be far from remarkable.

30 *Counterpoint* I, 189.

psychic operations. As noted, the operation of inversion, in combination with the operation of bounding, yields the affectual content of the fourth, and determines the particulars of its usage, and the same operation of inversion in combination with some unspecified operation we might provisionally term "thirdness" yields the very different affectual content of the sixth and the particulars of its usage.

Again, one might (justifiably) object that Schenker never develops an *ars combinatoria* of psychic operations sufficiently for it to stand truly as a theory of musical perception. Does the commonality of the operation of inversion in some way bind the perceptions of fourths and sixths? Does the same operation come into play in the case of seconds and sevenths, making, for example, the 7–6 suspension a perceptually more complex version of the 2–3 suspension? Or does it require other factors ("thirdness", for example) as a catalyst? Does it apply when particular affects defined in the counter-point are scaled-up in free composition? Regarding this latter operation, does the motion 1–2–4 in free composition simply carry the same affect as the motion 1–2–3 in the counterpoint, or do the operations of bounding and inversion also come into play (the outer tones of the motion in free composition defining a fourth)?

This is a strong criticism, one which we may suspect has shadowed this particular line of thought. (Schenker himself will eventually be given a chance to reply.) This under-development of the mechanics of the psychic operations, however, may (within the context of the economy of the first volume of *Counterpoint*) constitute not a weakness but a strength. In working from the thesis that the presence of a stratum of psychic operations serves to forestall any automatic reading of free composition as a series of affects isolable within the counterpoint, we are led to ask whether further development of the matrix of operations and their complexes would enhance or undercut this function. We arrive at a delicate, almost troubling answer: we think this under-development is convenient for Schenker, since even if a thorough and detailed hypothesis concerning the working of the psychic operations were available or even plausible, it would but displace the reduction of free composition to another level.

AN EPISTEMOLOGICAL CRISIS AND A PLAUSIBLE SOLUTION

We cannot but be uneasy with this answer, with its intimation that Schenker finds his theory to be in some manner dangerous to his general conception of music, and rather quietly leaves this theory incomplete. Perhaps our unease, though, is the key to a new insight on Schenker's situation.

Speaking pragmatically, we can see the exchange between the domain of psychic operations and the domain of psychological content in *Counterpoint* I mirrored in the exchanges among (or dependencies holding among) three distinct discursive modalities, three ways of reading counterpoint. At one extreme counterpoint reads as an intersubjective codification of the psychological content of musical figures. At another, it reads as a laboratory wherein the mechanics of musical perception are brought under scrutiny. At again another, it reads as a discipline which informs the examination of actual music.

Schenker seems comfortable with the stability of this discursive design, and the sense of equilibrium contained therein informs the delicate balance of the discussion of the content of figures with the use of these same figures to elucidate musical passages, and hence with the re-situation of theory proposed in his agenda. At the same time, this equilibrium of discourse suppresses any instabilities and imbalances: it masks the dissonance holding between that domain of the investigation that is least easily developed, namely the domain of the psychic operation, and those domains arrived at more fluidly, such as the elucidation of passages from free composition. Likewise it conceals a tension between those portions of the investigation that are (at least potentially) systematic and those portions inherently heuristic.

Moreover, Schenker's discursive design suppresses (although with less success) a lapse between his program and his execution. As noted, there is an epistemological argument embedded in Schenker's agenda: the hypothetical psychic operations made available under explanation (which the psychologist would hold to be verifiable in theory by objective experimental testing) are assumed to be embodied in that cultural artifact which is counterpoint (and which can be rigorously tabulated), and this mediating construct can, in turn, inform the way one speaks of actual passages (wherein musical intuitions are subjectively approached through a loose introspection). In practice, however, Schenker holds only loosely to this argument (as we would expect). He does not attempt to systematize the matrix of operations and their complexes within an autonomous domain, nor does he authentically take the opposing tack, laying out problematic passages from free composition and then attempting to discern the psychological–contrapuntal content of these passages rather than the other way around. (This point is admittedly ungenerous, as he does exactly this at times within his critical practice.) Perhaps most tellingly, he does not disinterestedly lay out his predecessors' observations (or the codification of these observations within the discipline of counterpoint) as evidence for a musical psychology, but instead inserts himself as an arbiter, screening (oftentimes for his own ends) these observations against the supposed authority of his own musical intuitions.

Again, we attribute, perhaps, an inappropriate intellectual theatricality to the historical Schenker. Yet there is a profit to be made in conceiving this seeming friction between argument and execution, this inability to conform to an epistemological program which authorizes the work, as the central problem of the post-*Counterpoint* I Schenker. Most immediately, it furnishes a convincing rationale for the disjunction between the two volumes of counterpoint. One conceives a Schenker who is aware of the lapse holding between the implicit agenda and its realization in *Counterpoint* I, who opts to remedy this lapse in *Counterpoint* II by jettisoning in its entirety his earlier epistemology, instituting instead in this latter work a more viable (if less radical) rigor derived solely from the taxonomy of the species.

Yet this conception of a central problem also makes available to our imaginations a hypothetical post-*Counterpoint* I Schenker who restores a measure of consistency to his investigation through quite the opposite strategy. (We would note, however, that this program conforms to the general expectations of theorists in the first decade of the century.) Such a Schenker would make psychological explanation an immediate goal in itself, he would construct a hypothetical matrix of psychic operations and their mechanics, and he would attempt to substantiate this matrix through a series of experiments or invented demonstrations or perhaps even argue their validity on the grounds of logical consistency.[31]

---

31 For example, in order to substantiate Schenker's notion of the psychological content of the fourth, the experimenter might play for the subject a sequence of simple intervals within the register of a single octave, ask the subject to evaluate each interval on a scale of tension and relaxation, and time the subject's responses. In evaluating this trial, the experimenter might disregard the responses given to dissonant intervals, disregard likewise the actual responses to consonant intervals, and see instead if there is any correlation between response time and interval. If Schenker's hypothesis of fourth recognition is true, this might show up as a slightly lengthened response time. To confirm any such correlation, the experimentalist might vary the timbre of the sequence of intervals, or vary their registral disposition, or vary the space between events in the experiment. A second experiment might begin with a chord or sonority, sounded only so loud and long as to cross the

The epistemological rationalization of theory set out by this Schenker would be anchored at one pole by a fixed and (at least hypothetically) empirically secure body of psychological explanation and at the other by the heuristic mapping of musical experience evidenced within received theory (music theory being taken as a special class of subjective observation) in combination with the structured introspective examination of that experience (and this examination would perhaps take priority over received theory).There would be a reciprocal exchange between these two investigations: psychological explanation would provide a defined collection of insights on which to ground the heuristic examination of pieces, while introspective examination of musical experience would come to provide the grounds upon which the hypothetical operation is to be both generated and verified.

This rethinking of the agenda and methodologies of music theory would promise potentially more than a clear appeal to scientific prestige. Most immediately, it would loosen theory from its pedagogical or prescriptive antecedents (a sort of theory destined not to make its appearance until mid-century), and could thus make strong claims to disciplinary priority, could situate itself anterior to both composition and the history of music. (This sort of anteriority is foreshadowed in Schenker's notion that a change in the practice of organum comes as a result of a collective sensitization to the psychological content of the fifth.)[32]

In other words, our fictional Schenker could assert his theory as the same sort of master-discourse for music as does the historical Schenker (or at least the Schenker of *Free Composition*). In this respect he comes closest to plausibility. However, when we come to envision in detail how the program of this fictional Schenker is to be carried through, we arrive at a rather different appreciation. He would certainly come to realize the difficulty, even the impossibility, inherent in the attempt to construct a mechanics of psychic operations not merely suggestive or rhetorically functional, or not

threshold of hearing, and then follow with a sequence of intervals, asking the subject to rate these intervals as to which is most characteristic of the sonority, and again timing the subject's response. A similar experiment might do the same for brief musical passages. Each of these experiments, of course, would be duplicated and varied. Inasmuch as the structural psychologists regarded perception as a complex of of sensation and image, one might imagine Schenker pursuing the definition of the "musical image." For a discussion of psychological protocols, see Kurt Huber, *Der Ausdruck musikalischer Elementarmotive: eine experimentalpsychologische Untersuchung* (Leipzig: J. A. Barth, 1923).The question of internal logic or consistency as the justification for a psychologistic theory is a touchy one at this time. See Riemann, "Ideen zu einer 'Lehre von den Tonvorstellungen.'"

32 *Counterpoint* I, 132–133.

merely verifiable, but sufficiently integrated and exhaustive as to anchor his entire discourse. It is one thing to posit such operations as "identity," "bounding," "grouping," "inversion," and the like, quite another to assume first that one has uncovered all such operations and second to assume that one can gauge or weigh or model their interactions.

He could also not but find himself in a methodological quagmire. To give this Schenker a certain measure of credit, we would grant him a healthy awareness of the dangers of an inappropriate selectivity and evaluation. In part, as we have noted, his recourse to received theory in *Harmony* and *Counterpoint* I gave access to a body of evidence which could be said to be exhaustive (within limits) and uncontaminated by personal biases. Even in these works, though, Schenker adjudicates received theory in terms of his own intuitions, and in the radical project which we have posited for our fictional Schenker, personal intuition would have to take not simply adjudicatory but methodological priority (in so far as harmony and counterpoint capture only limited areas of the musical experience). The notion of qualitative psychological evidence drawn from introspection is not (or not in Schenker's historic context) to be dismissed *a priori*.[33] Rather, it is the protocol governing this procedure which must be placed under question. If received theory constitutes a limited (and hence) inadequate ground from which to draw hypotheses, such hypotheses must instead be drawn in good part from introspection. Yet it is exactly here, under introspection, that such hypotheses must, to at least some degree, be verified. This problem is not insurmountable. But only with much work could one avoid the risk of placing too great a justificatory burden (however covertly) on the intuition of the investigator rather than on the design of the protocol. In fact, these two preceding problems are bound up together: theoretical adequacy and methodological justification are each to be subsumed under the general question of epistemological integrity. It is

---

33 The methodology of introspection in the opening decades of the twentieth century is truly ramified and elaborate. Wundt's protocol, analyzing the twin structures of sensation and feeling, evaluated the former along a three-dimensional scale of modality, intensity, and duration, and the latter in terms of the oppositions pleasure/displeasure, tension/relaxation, and excitement/depression. The structural psychologist adds the analysis of image to those of sensation and feeling. An excellent introduction to the structural psychologist's construction of introspective protocols (and the various controversies within the discipline) is found in Edward Titchener's *Lectures on the Experimental Psychology of the Thought-Processes* (New York: Macmillan, 1909; rpt. New York: Arno Press, 1973). Titchener, an American student of Wundt in Leipzig, became the dominant figure in structural psychology, founding the first American psychological laboratory at Cornell University. His writings on the whole are principally concerned with methodology.

on this point that our fictional Schenker must be seen to fail. The Schenker of *Counterpoint* I, masking an explanatory inadequacy underneath a discursive certainty, is forgivably culpable of a rhetorical sleight-of-hand. This Schenker could not but find himself engaged in defining his project rather than putting it through in practice, and were he to claim an empirically secured theory of music he would be less forgivably guilty of an act of bad faith.

A DESCRIPTIVE AND ANALYTIC PSYCHOLOGY

On the evidence provided by his later theory, though, we come to discover that the historical Schenker arrives at a rather different solution to his epistemological crisis.

For reasons of his own choosing, Schenker rarely returns in his later work to passages from free composition he has earlier examined. In *Free Composition*, however, he does revisit the anomalous close of Chopin's Mazurka, Op. 30, No. 4 which had ever so briefly figured into the discussion of parallel fifths in the first volume of *Counterpoint* (Ex. 1b).[34] In the counterpoint study, we remember, he uses this passage as a point from which to argue against the construal of the fifth as an acoustic doubling, asserting (implicitly) that the affect of this sequence derives from the repetition of the psychic operation of "bounding." Here, without any specific explanation, he reads Chopin's sequence (significantly preserving the distinction between parallel fifths and parallel octaves) as the condensation of a succession of 4–5 suspensions (Ex. 2).[35]

Example 2   Heinrich Schenker, *Free Composistion*, fig. 54/6

---

34 *Counterpoint* I, 133–134.

35 Heinrich Schenker, *Neue musikalische Theorien und Phantasien*, vol. III: *Der freie Satz* (Vienna: Universal Edition, 1935), trans. and ed. Ernst Oster as *Free Composition* (New York and London: Longman, 1979), fig. 54/6. All citations hereafter are to Oster.

Condensation, of course, has long been recognized by theorists as a valid compositional device. We need only recall Monteverdi's polemic or Kirnberger's explanation of triadic harmony. It is presented as an important feature of free composition in *Harmony* and *Counterpoint* I. In fact, in no more than a few pages following the discussion of parallel perfect consonances in the latter Schenker explains a passage of chromatically rising parallel thirds through just such a condensation, marvelling at "how rapidly our perception functions – how it rushes with lightning speed through so many intervening stages and grasps the abbreviation" (Ex. 3).[36]

Given this passage and its proximity to Schenker's digression on the nature of the fifth, we should be forgiven for locating an easy continuity between early and late readings of Chopin. Notions of condensation held respectively in *Counterpoint* I and *Free Composition* are subtly different, however. In the explication of the former, condensation is an operation automatic to the series of rising thirds in so much as the ear gauges this motion against a psychologically fixed diatonicism: two chromatic expansions of the diatonic background are concatenated in a rhythmically complex foreground (note that the exclamation points mark the trace of the diatonic background), and it is from this expansion that the (absent) surface is condensed. No such background obtains (immediately) for the condensed 4–5 suspensions of the latter: Schenker hears this condensation not in relation to some underlying diatonicism (although we know that this is remotely the case) but rather in relation to a contrapuntal formation. Phrased in the terms of *Counterpoint* I, Schenker would seem to be saying here that the affect of the parallel fifths derives from their condensation of contrapuntal motion. Yet in terms of the epistemology of *Counterpoint* I, this is a contradiction: a contrapuntal figure cannot itself come into play as part of an operation (or complex of operations) but can only constitute evidence of such. In other words, the logic of *Counterpoint* I does not allow a psychic operation (condensation) to operate on an affect (that affect isolated by the series of suspensions) to produce yet another affect (the sequence of parallel fifths).

Some other logic is at work here. Several pages earlier, *Free Composition* gives a sketch of the entire mazurka (Ex. 4).[37] We note two semitone

---

36 *Counterpoint* I, figs. 200 and 201, 148–149. The passage comes from Mozart's *Linz* Symphony. In accord with my general argument, I use "condensation" (with its psychological resonance) in preference to the rhetorical "abbreviation" or "ellipsis."

37 *Free Composition*, fig. 53/3.

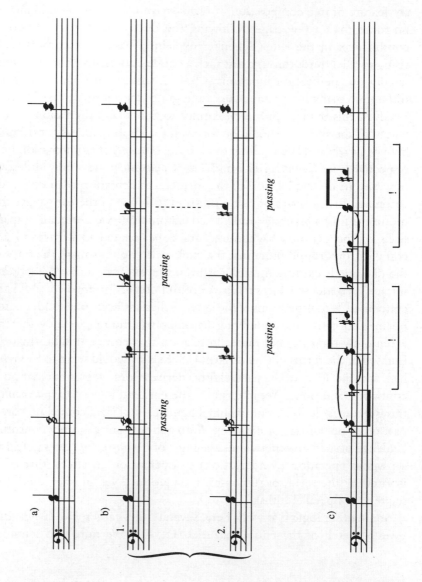

Example 3   Heinrich Schenker, *Counterpoint* I, fig. 201

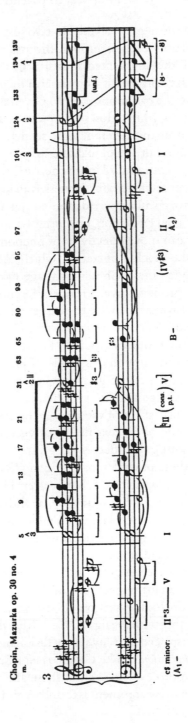

Example 4   Heinrich Schenker, *Free Composition*, fig. 53/3

descents (e–d♯ and a–g♯) bracketed in two places in the bass. We then note that this formation implies, through the assumption of a tonal retention, a 4–5 motion, the augmented fourth a/d♯ resolving to the fifth g♯/d♯. (This reading is reinforced if we conceive the preceding treble a♯ at m. 95 retained against the bass motion e–d♯.) Given this evidence, we realize that the condensation which closes the piece is an acceleration of a larger motion. Moreover, this different logic seems also to operate not simply at a local dimension but at a global one as well. In *Counterpoint* I, Chopin's curious passage is introduced into Schenker's text as an affectively autonomous musical moment. Its effectiveness as an illustration correlates directly with its status as a peculiarly vivid moment: it is in choosing a passage which in isolation so concretely concerns itself with the very sound of the fifth that Schenker can move directly from phenomenon to explication, from the affect to the psychic operation which makes for this affect. In *Free Composition*, by contrast, Chopin's passage does not, itself, ever make an appearance: we are never given the notes the composer has actually written. Of course we can ascribe this to the exigencies of Schenker's presentation; the reader is expected to consult the score. Yet even while holding these caveats in abeyance, one cannot help but sense that Schenker is making a rather subtle point through this mode of presentation. By rendering the actual surface of the music inconvenient, he ever so quietly frustrates a reading of the passage as a discrete phenomenal event. While he does not deny the particular affect of the passage, he seems (in making us refer to something outside of his text itself) to wish us to recognize the artifice involved in isolating this affect.

In concert, these observations give us a glimpse of the epistemological program of *Free Composition*. Schenker, rereading Chopin's passage, does not deny the affect of the sequence of fifths. The same psychological friction he attempts to explain in *Counterpoint* I through the immediate repetition of the psychic operation prompted by the fifth clearly prompts his reading of immediate condensations in *Free Composition*. In fact, the latter work even preserves the distinction drawn in the former between the psychological content respectively of the fifth and the octave: Schenker encloses the concluding section of the mazurka within parallel d♯–c♯ motions, indicating with the figure "8– –8" that there is no question of these octaves being displaced into any sort of dissonance-consonance formation. Yet in *Free Composition*, unlike *Counterpoint* I, Schenker acknowledges but does not attempt to explain each of these affects.

The key to his new argument is found in his treatment of counterpoint.

In *Counterpoint* I counterpoint is a laboratory within which musical affect can be isolated, and from which point hypotheses about the psychic operations underlying the affect can be generated: the contrapuntal figure, as a sort of affectual shorthand, is brought into proximity with free composition to show the predominance in that passage from free composition of a particular affect. In the task of the fictional Schenker put forward in the previous section, counterpoint loses its privileged position as the focus of the inquiry shifts to the verification of hypotheses of psychic operations: counterpoint cannot but become merely one class of evidence about the musical experience among a universe of evidence generated by introspection. *Free Composition* goes even farther, stripping counterpoint altogether of its status as a laboratory. By compensation, though, it does recapture its place within Schenker's program as the description of affect.

In other words, *Free Composition* suspends psychologistic explanation while preserving the notion of psychological content. Counterpoint is thus abstracted differently: still removed from its origin as a collection of compositional prescriptions, it takes on the role of descriptive convention, and as a convention or symbolic system rather than as evidence is itself subject to manipulation. It is this capacity to function as a calculus of affect that most tellingly distinguishes the counterpoint of *Free Composition* from that of its predecessors. The counterpoint of *Counterpoint* I, conceived as the evidence of psychological content, must be seen to assume tangibility as the product of a mechanics of psychic operations – the fourth, as we remember, is a product of "bounding" and "inversion." Thus, *Counterpoint* I would not, for example, read a sixth superimposed on a fourth to form a trichord as the simple product of three intervalic affects, but potentially as the product of "bounding" and "inversion" and "thirdness" and "inversion" again, and perhaps "dissonance" and "octave-displacement." The problem, in fact, with this reading would involve the identification of those operations which would come into play in hearing the trichord and the calculus wherein they are arrayed. It is this problem which our fictional Schenker would solve, but whose solution we would think beyond him. By contrast, the counterpoint of *Free Composition* would quite easily read the psychological product of this same trichord as, perhaps, the coincidence of two or more events or contrapuntal motions – every contrapuntal figure is always to be read in terms of other contrapuntal figures. In fact, Schenker most strikingly intuits that as an abstract representational system, counterpoint is not bound to any particular dimension, that every particular musical moment can only be described as a complex of differently spanned descriptions.[38] Hence, the depth of psychological operations and their complexes (which is intimated in *Counterpoint* I and becomes the object of an inevitably futile investigation in the fictional Schenker) comes to fruition as a depth of descriptive complexes in *Free Composition*: Psychological description comes to entail (in a way not available to psychological explanation) an analysis.

We arrive therefore at a more generous reading of *Counterpoint* II. Where before we had characterized the distance at which this work seems to hold itself from both *Counterpoint* I and *Free Composition* negatively, where we had characterized it in terms of the absence of an epistemology or as a temporary solution to the crisis in *Counterpoint* I, we might now see it holding the same relation to *Free Composition* and the remainder of Schenker's later analysis as the work of pure mathematics holds to the systems of physics. We might see it as an examination of some internal logic of counterpoint which, while not in any strict way determining the results of contrapuntal description, makes available a range of possibilities to that description.

We come to better understand Schenker's strong assertion in his later work that his analysis is to be taken as an art rather than a science. We would read this assertion broadly both as a means for Schenker to distance himself from the pretensions of contemporary theory and as a caution against the mechanistic application of his analysis. More specifically, though, we would read it as a declaration of the distance between his early psychologistic

---

38 We gain certain advantages by conceiving Schenker's analysis for the time being as an aggregate of partial readings gauged loosely by span rather than as a sequence of strata generated by a rule either of elaboration or disembellishment. While this move is in some respects counterintuitive, I believe that it insulates us from several very common interpretive errors. It is very tempting when conceiving the analysis as a sequence from musical surface through foreground and middleground to background (or vice versa) to read this sequence as embodying some decrease (or increase) in empirical content, or some increase (or decrease) in degree of abstraction. It is this conception which (even if unarticulated) allows, for example, some more pragmatic critics to acknowledge the insight and acuity of Schenker's foreground analyses while disallowing the background as an ideological construct. (Schenker's own mystification of the background is of no help in this regard.) It also, in a different way, encourages us to hypothesize a body of logical operations which govern the relations between strata of the analysis (perhaps as an epistemological compensation for a loss of empirical justification). I think that it is more profitable, however, to conceive Schenker's analytic strata as differing in scale rather than in substance or status. In other words, I do not believe that Schenker argues a background common to a large number of masterworks as a more abstract construction than the particular foreground of a musical text. Rather, the specific behaviors or the background, middleground, and foreground are argued as empirical generalizations derived from his examination of a large number of texts (although we would have justifiable doubts about the integrity of these generalizations).

epistemology, with its reliance on the method of natural science, and his later agenda, and also as a demand for an introspective integrity crucial to this later agenda.

We gain some insight into the disappearance (in Schenker's later work) of such classical problems of music theory as the status of the minor mode and the limits of the triadic construction of chords. While Schenker himself would probably indicate that such questions had been dealt with at sufficient length in his earlier work, we might argue that inasmuch as description must be congruent with the item described, such questions (like the notion of psychic operations) are easily, even necessarily, held in abeyance.

Likewise, we gain some insight into the dramatic subordination or suppression of harmony in Schenker's mature analysis. Rather obviously this is a means by which Schenker marks off his analysis from that of his competitors. Yet it was in harmony that an earlier generation of theorists had most eagerly sought to attack the foundations of a musical psychology. While Schenker will admit harmony to his analysis when it enhances his description of affect, he must (at least at the surface of his analysis) deny its status as a system.

Hence we come to place Schenker's solution in *Free Composition* to the problematic psychologism of his early theory within a larger intellectual context. To recapitulate, we would venture an intimate connection between the epistemological agenda of the first volume of *Counterpoint* (and *Harmony*) and that of *Free Composition*, that the assumptions which ground the latter work can only be understood as a response to the psychologistic assumption or assumptions of the former work (or works), that at some point in the trajectory linking Schenker's earlier and later theory the abstracted counterpoint of *Counterpoint* I, which had functioned as a systematic and communal body of musical intuitions giving evidence of the underlying mechanics of musical perception, is reconceived as a means of reporting personal musical intuitions from which can be inferred a general analysis of musical experience, and thus that *Free Composition* may be said to constitute a coherent and developed psychology of music. While we find it easy to grant at a distance Schenker's experiential claims (and indeed much has been made of the resemblance between Schenker's stratification and the mental models of language proposed by Chomsky), his articulation of these claims in *Free Composition* is so opaque, so arrogantly transcendental as to discourage us from discerning any trace of a psychological argument such as we would find in either constructivist theories of music (such as those of Kurth or Leonard Meyer) or theories that claim the sanction of empirical psychology (such as we have seen in Riemann).[39] Moreover, it must be granted that we have ventured this argument on the basis of a hasty, limited, and impressionistic survey of Schenker's writings. We would, however, suggest that this reading of Schenker commands a certain legitimacy when situated within the context of Dilthey's critique of psychologism and its ramifications within the general intellectual culture of the time.

We need not claim a specific causal link between Dilthey's essay and Schenker's program (nor would we be so naive as to demand such a link). We need not claim for Schenker an exaggerated place within the general reaction to Dilthey's critique. To make our case, we need but claim for Schenker's late analysis a kinship with the various strands of post-Dilthey

---

39 Both Kurth and Meyer draw on later psychological models, particularly those of the Gestalt psychologists (such as Koffka and Wertheimer) who were (with the behaviorists) at first competitors to, and later the most viable successors of, the post-Wundtian structural psychologists. See the portion of Kurth's *Grundlagen des linearen Kontrapunkts. Einführung in Stil und Technik von Bach's melodischer Polyphonie* (Bern: Max Drechsel, 1917; Berlin: Max Hesse, 1922, 1927); translated in Lee A. Rothfarb, *Ernst Kurth: Selected Writings* (Cambridge: Cambridge University Press, 1991). Rothfarb's introduction is particularly enlightening on the subject of Kurth's intellectual context. Schenker's notions of closure, grouping, and of foreground and background invite some comparison with the work of the Gestalt psychologist, yet I think that any such filiation of the former and latter would be deceptive. Schenker's psychology, as such, is fundamentally introspective, concerned with describing the experiential content of the passage, whereas the psychology of Koffka or Wertheimer is fundamentally distrustful of introspection and would certainly not be considered a descriptive psychology. For example, the Gestalt foreground and background are immediately given to perception. They are in fact fundamental to organizing perception, and can be demonstrated through the optical paradox wherein this organization (in a sense) turns on itself. One cannot conceive a corresponding aural illusion wherein the organization of Schenkerian foregrounds and backgrounds is called into question as a perceptual mechanism. (Such paradoxes can be constructed which bring into question our perception of octave assignment.) Much energy after the collapse of structural psychology was channelled into developmental psychology. See, for example, Leonhard Deutsch, *Individual-Psychologie im Musikunterricht und in der Musikerziehung: ein Beitrag zur Grundlegung musikalischer Gemeinkultur* (Leipzig: Steingräber, 1931). The parallel of Schenker's theory and Chomsky's transformational grammar is first drawn (to the best of my knowledge) in Milton Babbitt's "The Structure and Function of Music Theory" [1965] in *Perspectives on Contemporary Music Theory* ed. Benjamin Boretz and Edward T. Cone (New York, Norton, 1972), 10–21 (see in particular pp. 20–21). Chomsky's reconstitution of the notion of mental structures, his notion of deep structure embedded in language, provided perhaps the most important philosophical impetus to the rethinking of the notion of mind which is central to the cognitive psychology which displaced behaviorism. Eugene Narmour, in *Beyond Schenkerism: The Need for Alternatives in Musical Analysis* (Chicago: University of Chicago Press, 1977) attacks Schenker in part through a parallel critique of transformation or generative grammer. Fred Lerdahl and Ray Jackendoff's *A Generative Theory of Tonal Music* (Cambridge, Mass. and London: MIT Press, 1983) presents itself as a correction of Schenker's theory.

psychologism. Of course this kinship is not one of reach or ambition or purpose. Dilthey's projected descriptive and analytic psychology, with its internal structures of perception, volition and the like could not (if realized) but prompt a rather different and undoubtedly broader investigation of music: the character of such an investigation we can perhaps glimpse if we imagine (let us say) a Freudian or Husserlian study of music. It is rather a family resemblance of method or epistemology. Without question (to continue the comparison) the intense and highly theorized scrutiny of verbal artifacts involved in Freud's analysis and the rigid introspective bracketing of Husserl's phenomenology constitute methods of description quite different than that of the superimposition of notationally commensurable and dimensionally distinct descriptions of Schenker's analysis, yet each constitutes a descriptive protocol. And while Freud arrives at a functional structure of consciousness, Husserl a structure of perception, Schenker arrives at what we need to think of as a structure of musical perception in the substantive reconciliation of the complex of descriptions.

THE HISTORIOLOGICAL IMPERATIVE

THE AUTHORITY OF HISTORY

Lest we become too comfortable with a psychologistic *Free Composition*, we need observe that Schenker's analysis could likewise be read in terms of a second, perhaps even more ramified engagement with the later nineteenth-century sciences of music, the beginnings of which are to be found in an essay roughly contemporaneous with *Harmony* and *Counterpoint* I. Schenker's *A Contribution to the Study of Ornamentation* stands as a companion piece to his critical edition of C. P. E. Bach's keyboard works.[1] As in the respective prefaces to its two theoretic siblings, Schenker moves quickly in the opening of *Ornamentation* to differentiate his work from that of his predecessors, casting himself as the champion of C. P. E. Bach's keyboard writing against a certain school of false or naive historicism.[2] His primary target is von Bülow's venerable edition of several of the keyboard works.[3] In accord with a general notion that because of the nature of Bach's instrument, the clavichord, these works are excessively parsimonious in their sonority, over-extravagant in their embellishment and in general under-notated, von Bülow thickens textures through the addition of inner voices and harmonic supports, simplifies the melodic line through the

---

1 Heinrich Schenker, *Ein Beitrag zur Ornamentik, als Einführung zu Ph. Em. Bach's Klavierwerken mitumfassend auch die Ornamentik Haydns, Mozarts, Beethovens etc.* (Vienna: Universal, 1904; 2nd edn. 1908). Translated by Hedi Siegel as "A Contribution to the Study of Ornamentation" in *Music Forum* 4 (New York: Columbia University Press, 1976), 11–139. All page citations will be to this translation, hereafter refered to as *Ornamentation*. This study constitutes a critical companion to C. P. E. Bach, *Klavierwerke*, ed. Heinrich Schenker (Vienna: Universal, 1902).

2 *Ornamentation*, 11–20.

3 Carl Philipp Emanuel Bach, *Sechs ausgewählte Sonaten für Klavier allein*, ed. Hans von Bülow (Leipzig: C. F. Peters, 1862). This edition was reissued several times by Peters (under the title *Sechs Klavier-Sonaten*) through 1928 (most germanely in 1902). Schenker also refers to the more scholarly (but also inadequate) C. P. E. Bach, *Clavier-Sonaten, Rondos und freie Fantasien für Kenner und Liebhaber*, ed. E. F. Baumgart (Breslau: F. E. C. Leuckart, 1863).

deletion of ornament, and clarifies the whole through the addition of dynamic and articulative markings. Schenker, needless to say, takes von Bülow to task on each of these points, arguing that Bach's sonorities are fully capable of standing on their own; that inasmuch as Bach by his own admission notated every ornament quite deliberately, each must be taken as intrinsic to the continuity of the work as a whole, and that the dynamic and articulative markings as originally given convey all necessary information without cluttering the page.[4]

Passing over the detail of Schenker's program for the moment, we would grant *Ornamentation* a delicate and important place in Schenker's development inasmuch as his assertions lead easily to the account of the history of music to which he will hold (with little elaboration) in the remainder of his writings. As we recall, he will come to see the unique nature of the instrumental medium as a hinge on which a great dialectical motion turns, wherein the sweep of Renaissance vocal counterpoint and the instrumental practice of the seventeenth and eighteenth centuries are synthesized in the hands of the German masters of the late eighteenth and nineteenth centuries, where the horizontal and vertical in music are themselves brought into balance.[5]

---

4   *Ornamentation*, 21–27. Schenker's argument is more complex than this summary would indicate. (Some of these complexities will be drawn out later.) The next section of the essay (pp. 27–44) takes on the issues of form and tonality and closes with an examination of each specific composition in Schenker's edition. (The discussion of the technique of "group formation" is particularly fascinating.) The following section discusses performance (pp. 44–49): Schenker specifically recommends a comparatively slow tempo and a detached touch. The concluding section of the essay deals sequentially with the ornamental typology of C. P. E. Bach's *Versuch*, discussing in turn and at length the substance and execution of the long appoggiatura, the short appoggiatura, the trill, the turn, and the turn after a note (pp. 51–139). Interestingly, each discussion begins with an explication of the "psychology" of the particular ornament, a notion which ties this work to its contemporaries, *Harmony* and *Counterpoint* I. The "psychological content" Schenker locates within these ornaments is usually a suspension–resolution motion.

5   Schenker gives several historical accounts in *Harmony*. The longest and perhaps most interesting explicit historical narrative, wherein he develops the notion of an increasing awareness of the organizing powers of harmony is on pp. 163–173. He first ascribes the invention of polyphony to composers frustrated by liturgical limitations placed on the length of musical pieces, then speaks of how the desire for fuller sonorities within these constraints comes to constrict the melodic invention of music, and finally sees music liberated by the monody of Peri and Caccini to seek its own breadth and bring harmony under control through the subsumption of the scale-step. He turns to the rather different argument given here, however, and holds to it in the remainder of his writings. The historical narrative contained within *Counterpoint* I stands almost as a transition between these two narratives (pp. xxv–xxviii). Schenker's later argument, in *Free Composition*, turns (as we would expect) on the notion of diminution (pp. 93–96). See also his treatments of the origins of repetition and of the scale degree (pp. 99, 111).

More simply put, Schenker's early concern with ornamentation takes its place (in his later analysis) as a theory of diminution. Indeed, *Free Composition* resembles nothing so much in appearance as the late sixteenth-or seventeenth-century diminutional treatise.[6] We might hesitate, though, to draw any substantive or epistemological link between the agenda of *Ornamentation* and that of *Free Composition*. While we can, with some confidence, speak of *Ornamentation* as historiographic in its method and agenda, we would be justifiably cautious about speaking of Schenker's mature analysis as in some fundamental way engaged with the investigations of the historian. In fact, the historical account we have noted would appear more a way of containing or marginalizing the historical sciences than a way of embracing or incorporating these sciences. We would find it difficult actually to equate the diminution of *Free Composition* with objectively historical diminutional practices; we would not expect actually to locate a seventeenth-century diminutional treatise whose figures correspond to those of *Free Composition*. The assertion that any of Schenker's work embodies substantively a real concern with the historiography of music would seem implausible.[7]

But this is precisely the assertion we would make. We would argue that in a distinct and specific (if covert) manner Schenker's later analysis makes historiological claims, that it is a product of a recoverable engagement not

6   This is simply an impression. It is interesting to compare such widely separated treatises. See in particular Sylvestro Ganassi, *Opera intitulata Fontegara* [1535], ed. and Ger. trans. Hildemarie Peter (Berlin-Lichterfelde: Robert Lienau, 1956), Eng. trans. Dorothy Swainson (Berlin-Lichterfelde: Robert Lienau, 1959). Ganassi sets out a graded series of diminutions for every primary melodic interval. It is particularly interesting that he regards the pitches of these melodic intervals as pitch classes. A diminution from (let us say) c to d may span a second or also a ninth. Schenker would be familiar with the musicological treatment of diminution, such as Adolph Beyschlag's *Die Ornamentik der Musik* (Leipzig: Breitkopf und Härtel, 1908). Robert Haas's *Aufführungspraxis der Musik* (Wildpark-Potsdam: Akademische Verlagsgesellschaft Athenaion, 1931) is specifically cited by Schenker (*Free Composition*, 94).

7   Granted, Schenker ties his project to the historical diminutional practice of Fux's counterpoint and also to the thoroughbass schools of the eighteenth century (*Counterpoint* I, xxvii–xxviii). As argued earlier, this filiation may be important as a return to a music theory within which there was no distinction between the speculative and the practical. Schenker is less conscious of the historical placement of species counterpoint than some of his contemporaries, however. While a pedagogical distinction between sixteenth- and eighteenth-century counterpoints lies almost two decades beyond *Counterpoint* I (a distinction we might attribute to Kurth's counterpoint), there is a circle of Catholic writers around F. X. Haberl who at the turn of the century reify Palestrina's contrapuntal practice. See P. Griesbacher, *Kirchenmusikalische Stilistik und Formenlehre*. I. Historischer Teil (Regensburg: Albert Coppenrath, 1912–16) and Wilhelm Hohn, *Der Kontrapunkt Palestrinas und seiner Zeitgenossen: eine Kontrapunktlehre mit praktischen Aufgaben*. Sammlung "Kirchenmusik," vol. XVII (Regensburg: Pustet, 1918).

necessarily or simply with his own rather fixed account of the history of music but with the methodology of the later nineteenth-century historical sciences. To substantiate this assertion, we must look not to how he addresses, in particular, the idealized domain of the history of music, but rather to the manner in which he addresses two related and more pragmatic domains, respectively, those of editing and performance – and to do so, we need look more closely at *Ornamentation*.

THE IMPROVISATORY IMAGINATION, EDITING, EXECUTION

While *Ornamentation* does contain a latent history, we must not forget that this is a work principally concerned with editorial procedure. Schenker works from the assumption that the masterwork does not allow any sort of editorial correction that is justified on the basis of a theoretic or historicist rationale, that the masterwork resists being updated. Thus, he rejects the reregistration of Bach's sonorities for the modern piano, as well as the supposed clarification of melodic lines.

This stance is in itself perhaps unremarkable. Schenker, however, feels that he must take things further, that he must deal theoretically with the issue of embellishment. In the central section of *Ornamentation* he removes his discourse to a more philosophical domain. He asserts that the editorial misappropriation of Bach's text is bound up with a theoretical misperception of Bach's creative process. He argues that Bach's art (and, by extension, that of the masters in general) is essentially an art of improvisation and as such resists being understood according to any schematic formulae: the editor's error is mirrored by the theorist's error, the false thickening of sonorities and the inappropriate deletion of melodic ornament are mirrored by the misapplied analysis of Bach's continuities by means of formal typologies.[8]

Beet

---

8 *Ornamentation*, 27–28. Schenker's fixation on the practice of improvisation runs throughout his work. His discussion of modulation in *Harmony* concludes with an analysis of two unmeasured fantasias of C. P. E. Bach (pp. 339–341). The investigation of ostensibly "improvisatory" pieces is picked up in "The Art of Improvisation" in *Das Meisterwerk in der Musik*, I (Munich, Drei Masken Verlag, 1925), 9–40, ed. and trans. William Drabkin as *The Masterwork in Music: A Yearbook*, I (Cambridge: Cambridge University Press, 1994), 2–19. He returns to the importance of improvisatory practice in *Der freie Satz* (*Free Composition*, 6–7). It is not beyond belief that Schenker's reification of improvisation has some relation to his distrust of the discourse of musical form. The chapter in the *Harmonielehre* entitled "On Form on a Larger Scale" provides a trenchant critique of contemporary notions of form (*Harmony*, 241–250). He goes on in his analysis of C. P. E. Bach

Beet

The agency of the improvisatory imagination stands thus as a correction to both inappropriate editing and inappropriate analysis and in some idealized way straddles the domains of both historiography and theory. Construed as a general creative faculty, this improvisatory imagination would not seem open to systematization or analysis. Yet inasmuch as Schenker awards it a historical particularity, we might imagine him construing it as an activity among a family of activities open to scrutiny. Inasmuch as improvisation (unlike notated composition) is a form of performance, we can imagine Schenker investigating it as a sort of performance.

As previously noted, the notion of performance figures pragmatically in Schenker's conception of editing: he specifically rules out the dynamic and articulative emendation of Bach's text. Yet at one remove, if performance as a creative activity resists empiricization or theorization (all nineteenth-century attempts to develop a psychology notwithstanding), performance as an interpretive activity has, by the time of *Ornamentation*, become the subject of extensive and systematic consideration.[9] Holding pride of place among the various attempts to systematize the mechanics of giving voice to the surface represented by the score is (as we would expect) Riemann, who introduces a collection of plausible, finite, and (to his own mind) psychologically normative strategies for

to demonstrate that certain passages derive their coherence from tonality, or rhythm or the dynamics of light and shade rather than from some mechanical application of thematic returns (*Ornamentation*, 28–31).

9 The later nineteenth-century performance treatise differs markedly from its predecessors of the later eighteenth and early nineteenth centuries. This new genre of writings may have developed in part as a reaction to the mechanical exercise manuals of the earlier portion of the century. It certainly arises in conjunction with a methodic study of rhythm. See Rudolph Westphal, *Allgemeine Theorie der musikalischen Rhythmik seit J. S. Bach* (Leipzig: Breitkopf und Härtel, 1880), which applies classical prosodic theory to the interpretation of music. See also his defense of this reading against Riemann's critique serialized in "Die C-Takt-Fugen des Wohltemperierten Claviers" in the *Musikalisches Wochenblatt* 14 (1883), 237–238, 253–254, 265–267, 278–280, 289–291, 301–303, 313–315, 325–329. Theodor Weihmayer's *Musikalische Rhythmik und Metrik* (Magdeburg: Heinrichshofen, 1917) summarizes late nineteenth-century rhythmic theory and its relation to performance. Further discussions of performance are found in Mathis Lussy's well-known *Traité de l'expression musicale* (Paris: Berger-Levrault and Heugel, 1874) which leads into *Le Rhythme musicale* (Paris: Heugel, 1883) and Adolphe Carpé's interesting *Grouping, Articulation, and Phrasing in Musical Interpretation* (Leipzig: Bosworth, 1898) which likewise is related to his *Der Rhythmus* (Leipzig, Gebrüder Reinecke, n.d.). A different (but related) strain of thought is represented by Carl Fuchs's *Die Zukunft des musikalischen Vortrags* (Danzig: A. W. Kafemann, 1884) and Franz Kullak's *Der Vortrag in der Musik am Ende des 19. Jahrhunderts* (Leipzig: F. E. C. Leuckart, 1898).

"playing musically."[10] We need not rehearse these strategies in too much detail: music is constructed in accord with a norm of eight-measure units, partitioned equally into antecedent and consequent units; each four-measure unit divides into a pair of antecedent–consequent relations, with a stress falling on the second and fourth measures; and most locally, this dialectic maps onto the upbeat preparation to the agogic accent (which usually coincides with the bar line). For Riemann, to play musically involves an automatic or intuitive sensitivity to this innate rhythmic structure.

We might question the mechanical application of this construct, but we cannot deny its historical success. On the one hand, this success stems from the very simplicity of Riemann's theory, from a certain peda-gogical efficiency; on the other hand from the discursive economy of the nineteenth century. Loosely sketched, we would note that consequent to the specification of a canon, a substantial distance seems to open between the transcendent composer and the performer (particularly the amateur performer) that would seem to require a mediation. The score itself is taken as an incomplete or inefficient record of the composer's voice, necessitating the interpretive interpolation of an editor (most often a major performer such as Czerny or Busoni). Riemann theorizes this mediation, in effect, rationalizing the performance edition through a system of editorial notation (phrase slurs, measure functions, "real" bar lines) which brings the true voice of the composer to the surface of the score.

Schenker, as we have seen, castigates the casual emendation of articula-tory and dynamic markings in *Ornamentation*. He treats this same issue at greater length in an intriguing (if rambling) essay perhaps fifteen years later

10 Hugo Riemann's performance program is first definitively formulated in his *Musikalische Dynamik und Agogik: Lehrbuch der musikalischen Phrasirung* (Hamburg: D. Rahter, 1884), and later disseminated through a substantial number of short pedagogical and analytic works and through a series of "phrased editions." As has been the case, Riemann's ideas about interpretation are closely bound to his ideas about rhythm. See his *System der musikalischen Rhythmik und Metrik* (Leipzig: Breitkopf und Härtel, 1903). By the turn of the century Riemann's ideas about phrasing and weighting had come to seem somewhat inadequate or even mechanical. See Wiehmayer's *Musikalische Rhythmik*, Carpé's *Grouping* and Kullak's *Der Vortrag*. For a comparison of various examples of phrasing see Martin Frey, "Musikalisch-kritische Untersuchungen" in *Die Musik* 8/21 (August 1909), 171–181. See also Karl Zuschneid, "Das Phrasierungsproblem und die Konkurrenzausgaben von Klavierwerken" in the *Neue Zeitschrift für Musik* 79 (8, 12 August 1912), 451–454, 478–481. Riemann's ideas about performance have continued to have a certain presence, particularly in such later rhythmic formulations as hypermeasure and structural downbeats.

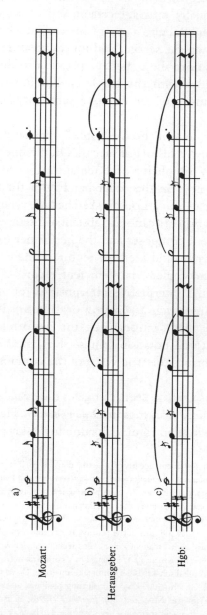

Ex. 5   Heinrich Schenker, "Abolish the Phrasing Slur," p. 21

entitled "Abolish the Phrasing Slur."[11] Again, he starts from the notion that the score is not to be taken as an approximation of the composer's intention (which can be sharpened through editorial intention) but as the exact representation of that intention manifested in terms of what we must assume to be a perfectly replete symbolic system. As the title indicates, though, he most directly addresses the central tool of the performance editor: the phrase slur. He first draws a distinction between the legato slur (a legitimate device of the composer) and the phrase slur (an exercise in editorial presumption). The legato slur (by reference to his standard historical account) descends from the grouping by word or syllable in Renaissance vocal composition.[12] This ligation survives through the period of instrumental diminution on vocal models and coalesces as a syntactic function in the work of the later eighteenth- and nineteenth-century masters. The phrase slur is, by contrast, an artificial creation, an attempt to impose an abstract, over-obvious unity on the already replete notation of the masterwork.

Schenker illustrates this difference in a subtle, slightly puzzling example (Ex. 5).[13] He gives three versions of the theme of Mozart's Rondo (K.485). The first (5a) is that given by Mozart; the latter two (5b and c) are taken from different performance editions (although Schenker does not supply any attributions). Of this latter pair of recensions, the first illustrates a capricious extension of Mozart's legato slur, the second a full-fledged phrase slur. In order to discredit these latter two recensions, Schenker very closely and insightfully argues Mozart's text. He points out that Mozart draws attention to the parallel arpeggiations of the first two measures by notating the passing tones of the first measures as appoggiaturas (a

---

11 "Abolish the Phrasing Slur," *The Masterwork in Music* I, 20–30. Only the opening portion of this essay deals with the phrase slur. One suspects that it may date from the period before the war in as much as there seem to be no other discussions of phrasing in the post-war German literature. Jonas reports the existence of an unpublished *Lehre des Vortrags* among the papers Schenker left at his death (*Free Composition*, xv.). Schenker speaks later of the same matters saying: "I should like to add here that the editors' predilection for phrase marks clearly indicates that even they, in the midst of the foreground, sense background relationships. But precisely in the foreground, diminution has to go its own way with its own articulation which diverges from that at earlier levels. (Also it is technically impossible to show in the foreground the slurs of all levels. A differentiation such as the small and large notation mentioned in §252, permitting middleground elements to be shown in the representation of the foreground, is out of the question for articulation, since there can be only one kind of slur.)" (*Free Composition*, 110–111).

12 "Abolish the Phrasing Slur," 20–21. This account of the history of music is notably closer to those of *Der freie Satz* than to those of the *Harmonielehre*.

13 "Abolish the Phrasing Slur," 21.

parallelism which survives in the first editorial recension but is masked in the second). To avoid making too much of an obviously flawed perfect parallelism, Mozart executes the most minimal of moves, adding the legato slur of the second measure. In effect, this slur functions as an acceleration compressing the three-count unfolding of the initial third of the first measure into a two-count echo in the second measure; it brings (to perception) a background rhythm – the implied ♩♩♩ of the first measure giving way to the implied ♩♩♩ of the second measure. The second measure is thus heard receding from the first and, in particular, the g♮ opening the second measure recedes from, is even subsumed by, the a♮ which opens the first measure. Thus, to alter Mozart's original articulation is to lose the depth of the passage.

Having made the case for Mozart's original text, Schenker then feels secure to venture several surprisingly concrete observations. He notes that in performance Mozart's hand moves five times in the first two measures. In the second version of the theme, the performer's hand moves four times. Yet in the third version, the performer's hand moves but once. Here the folly of the editor is taken to its extreme: in his zeal to impose a unity on Mozart's diversity, the editor's phrase slur, spanning the entire two measures, does not enliven but actually deadens the performance.

In the manner above cited, Schenker demonstrates how theory quite smoothly moves to performance. Something, though, gives us pause. Schenker's move is deceptive. In this last passage he overplays his hand. He predicates his essay on a distinction between the legato slur and the phrase slur (although, significantly, he never quite brings himself to define the phrase slur, assuming that the reader is familiar with the notion, perhaps even assuming that the reader shares his contempt). Yet when it comes time to speak of the actual physical entailments, Schenker reads the two slurs identically. We know this is not the case.

Schenker, as previously noted, does not attribute this second reading to anyone in particular, but it takes little imagination to properly assign it to Riemann or in all likelihood a disciple or admirer of Riemann. The phrase slur must, then, be taken as a complex notational convention. Another editor (one imagines Westphal in particular) might, in notating such a slur, expect a perfect legato, might even, in Schenker's own terms, demand a single motion of the hand. Riemann suggests not a simple articulation, though, but rather a higher-level analytic structure of agogic accents (to be placed on the second and fourth measures) and their preparations. The actual performance of such a structure would involve not the subsumption of everything under the slur in a single hand motion but a dynamic inflection. We would expect Riemann to require slight swells in the first and third measures, a pair of brief caesuras over the second and fourth barlines, and a dynamic recession (to borrow Schenker's term) in the second and fourth bars. Despite the erasure of Mozart's original markings, this reading is not so totally impoverished as Schenker would have us believe.[14]

Indeed, the disagreement between Schenker and Riemann is not particularly over results, but over the economy of performance. Under Riemann's regime, the score is taken to be inefficient, embedded in a matrix of assumptions external to itself which are held (if not articulated) by the composer, a matrix that the performer must reconstruct: hence, the figure of the editor or teacher stands as a necessary mediator. Riemann demands a canny performance. Schenker, by contrast, demands an uncanny performance. Under his regime the score is replete and the performer is overtly asked for nothing beyond fidelity to the text. He does not relinquish the substantive notion of performance, however; he does not simply assume a textual transparency. Rather, he situates this performance (or the dynamics of this performance – such as precession and recession) within the text itself.

In other words, while we may conceive of performance as an activity embodying certain mechanics, as a translation of notation into sound that we (may) find transparent (in accord with modernist dicta) or problematic (in accord with the post-modern equation of translation with interpretation), Schenker, in common with most late nineteenth- and early twentieth-century musicians, conceives it as involving a third agent, immanent and autonomous – something which transcends execution. He conceives

---

14 The Schenker of Der freie Satz would undoubtedly hear the same recession although he would explain it differently: a structural third-span from a through f♯ would locate the mediating g at the opening of the third measure rather than that of the second. It is interesting that in this early treatment Schenker does not ever call our attention to the parallel of two-measure units. In a way, this parallel is too obvious for Schenker to note (although it would not be too obvious for his predecessors). It is more interesting to think, however, that he is uncomfortable with this parallel, that he feels the first and second measures differently than he feels the third and fourth measures, yet is unable to articulate his intuitions. This second recension of Mozart's theme (the recension with the extended phrase slurs) assumes a nested matrix of weighted and unweighted: the relation between the first and second measures (and likewise the third and fourth measures) is mirrored in the relation between the two halves of the phrase. In other words, the agogic accent on the opening of the fourth measure is assumed to carry more weight than that of the second. In this way, this reading (with its implied Riemannian hypermeasure) is perhaps even closer to what we might attribute to the mature Schenker as mentioned above.

Example 6   J. S. Bach, subject of the C minor fugue from *Das wohltemperierte Klavier* edited by Hugo Riemann in
(a) C. Czerny   (b) R. Franz and O. Dressel   (c) Béla Bartók (reproduced by permission of Editio Musica Budapest)

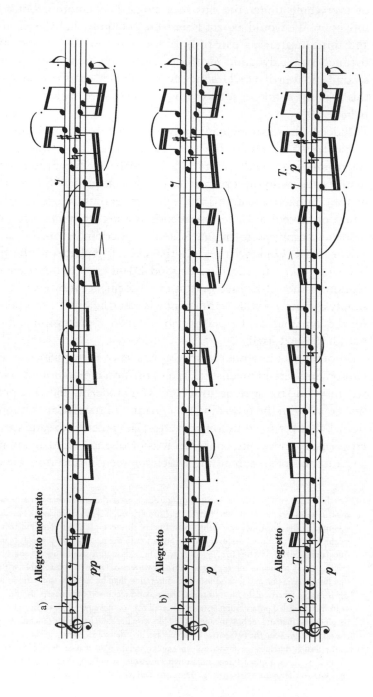

of this agency as a presence, or a voice which (ideally) binds composer and performer: i.e., the correct interpretation is not that which is most self-effacing, not that which is most willful, but that which captures this presence. Hence, Schenker's insistence on fidelity to the text cannot be taken as a prescription for erasing the performer, as a means of problematizing performance, or as a rejection of the transcendent performance, but as a reintegration of the fractured economy holding among composer, editor and performer (assumed by his contemporaries).

THE INTERIOR PERFORMANCE

We might speak of the immanent performative voice as an "interior performance." As yet, however, we cannot treat this notion as more than a working hypothesis. To put it to the test, to give it substance, we need to compare more directly the performance edition with Schenker's analysis. Thus, we turn to a familiar, convenient, and curiously slippery musical passage – the subject of J. S. Bach's C minor fugue from the first book of the *Well-tempered Clavier*. Three readings of this subject give us some idea of the complexity and detail of the notion of performance (Ex. 6a–c).[15] All three readings agree substantively through the middle of the second measure (excepting the second reading's lack of three slurred staccatos) and are, in fact, in accord with the importance of the second-measure a♭. The second reading clarifies the first's implicit swell to this a♭. The third reading is quirky, almost fussy: the editor obviously wishes to separate the f–g slide from the following a♭, indicating a slight caesura by means of the staccato articulation of f and g and the abrupt stress on a♭, yet in practice this separation would seem almost overplayed or mannered.

The idiosyncrasies of this reading begin to make sense, however, when

---

15 Johann Sebastian Bach, (1) *The Well-Tempered Clavichord* I, ed. C. Czerny (Boston: G. Schirmer, 1893), 10–11; (2) *Das wohltemperirte Klavier* I, ed. Robert Franz and Otto Dressel (Leipzig: Breitkopf und Härtel, 1890), 10–11; (3) *Das wohltemperierte Klavier* I, ed. Béla Bartók (Budapest: Zenemükiadó Vállalat, 1967), 30–31. There are numerous late nineteenth- and early twentieth-century interpretive readings of this subject. Westphal, for example, reads the subject as an anapest, and sees this rhythm reflected throughout the fugue (*Allgemeine Theorie*, 268–279). Two of the more interesting editions are *Die Fugen des wohltemperierten Klaviers: partiturmässig dargestellt und nach ihrem Bau erläutert* I, ed. F. Stade (Leipzig: Steingräber-Verlag, n.d.) and *Das wohltemperierte Klavier* I, ed. Ferruccio Busoni (Wiesbaden: Breitkopf und Härtel, n.d.), the first of which presents the fugues by voices and whose sole articulative marking is the phrase slur, and the second of which presents various fantastic augmentations of Bach's text. Schenker speaks of Busoni's edition in his essay. The Urtext of the fugue would have been available from the Bach-Gesellschaft by the fourth quarter of the nineteenth century.

Example 7   J. S. Bach, subject of the C minor fugue edited by Hugo Riemann in
         (a) *Grosse Kompositionslehre*
         (b) *Analysis of J. S. Bach's Wohltemperirtes Clavier*

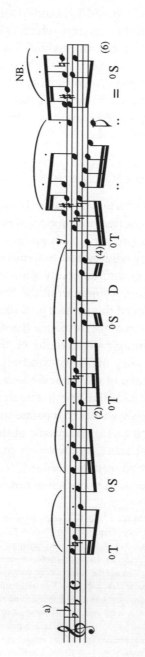

we examine two further readings (Ex. 7a–b).[16] Both are by Riemann – therefore we assume his performance rules: the staccati beneath the slurs of the first reading (7a) make it quite apparent that we are seeing an interpretive phrase slur rather than a normal articulative slur. Riemann's first reading (which might be designated an "analytic" reading) gives the placement of the principal agogic accents (the notations "2" and "4").Yet there is something slightly troubling in this reading. Where we would expect a phrase slur carrying to the third agogic accent, carrying to f, we are given instead an elongated slur which almost subsumes the entire second measure. Yet the third agogic stress on f is marked by a change of harmony. Yet again, the succeeding a♭ is likewise marked by the appearance of the dominant. Riemann's second reading (which might be designated an "executory" reading) further complicates matters. He dispenses with the phrase slur, or conceives it as a very local dynamic: the agogic stresses are articulatively marked, the subsidiary odd stresses further emphasized by the hairpin dynamics, and the principal stresses marked by measure position (with the "2" and "4"). Again, though, the second measure is problematic. Riemann appears to read this measure in two ways simultaneously. The third agogic stress on f is marked articulatively and dynamically, yet he seems to break down this emendation, dispersing the stress/staccato marking of the earlier agogic stresses over both f and g and delaying the decrescendo until after the sounding of a♭. At the same time, however, f and g are distinguished (because of their articulations) from the succeeding a♭, which is subsumed under a slur that may or may not be a phrase slur. (Interestingly, even in this reading Riemann groups the entire second measure of the countersubject together in a single span.)

Against the background of Riemann's theorized performances, the third member of the initial trio of readings (Bartók: 6c) comes into focus. We realize that the editor has internalized Riemann's performance rules while at the same time sharing with his two predecessors the conviction that the a♭ of the second measure is somehow the key to the entire passage and somehow needs to be stressed.[17] He undermarks the framework of agogic

16 (1) Hugo Riemann, *Grosse Kompositionslehre*, II (Berlin and Stuttgart: W. Spemann, 1903), 129. (2) Riemann, *Analysis of J. S. Bach's Wohltemperirtes Clavier* Part 1, trans. J. Shedlock (London: Augener, 1893), 11–14.

17 This understanding is confirmed when we read farther into Bartók's edition and discover additional examples of Riemann's reading marks and (at the end) a "real" barline rectifying the notational displacement of the final sounding of the fugue's subject (Bartók's edition is the most heavily emended edition in circulation – with the possible exception of that of Busoni). Although we have

Example 8   Heinrich Schenker's analysis of the subject of the
C minor fugue in "The Organic in the Fugue"

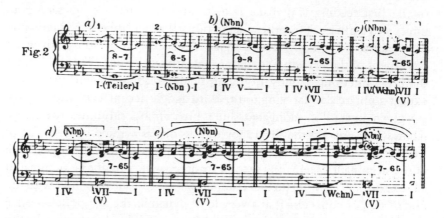

stresses, or marks them simply with staccati, and instead concentrates on the
point where the passage becomes problematic, setting the stressed a♭ apart,
emphasizing the way it upsets the mechanical uniformity of the passage.

But even more, it is against the background of this whole complex of
editorial readings that Schenker's own curiously elaborate derivation of the
fugue subject emerges as something quite different from what we would,
at first, think (Ex. 8a–f).[18] Schenker claims for his reading a true economy,

no indication of when Bartók put together his edition, we would note the survival of a Riemannian
tradition of performance in Central Europe. It is also interesting to note that Bartók reorders the
preludes and fugues, supposedly by difficulty. The C minor prelude and fugue are preceded by the
G major, D minor, B♭ major, E minor, A minor and F major preludes and fugues, and followed
immediately by the E major and F♯ major preludes and fugues.

18 Heinrich Schenker, "Das Organische der Fuge, aufgezeigt an der C-moll-Fuge aus dem
Wohltemperierten Klavier von Joh. Seb. Bach" in *Das Meisterwerk der Musik*, II (Munich: Drei
Masken Verlag, 1926) 55–95; trans. Hedi Siegel as "The Organic in the Fugue" in *The Masterwork
in Music: A Yearbook*, II, ed. William Drabkin, trans. Ian Bent, John Rothgeb, William Drabkin, Hedi
Siegel (Cambridge: Cambridge University Press, 1996). Another translation of Schenker's
treatment of the fugue subject is found in Maury Yeston's *The Stratification of Musical Rhythm* (New
Haven: Yale University Press, 1976), 59–62. All citations hereafter are to the translation. Much of
the work on Bach's fugues from around the time of Schenker's essay addresses the definition and
history of the fugue as a genre. For example, see Joseph Müller-Blattau, *Grundzüge einer Geschichte
der Fuge* (Königsberg: K. Jüterbock, 1923) and Reinhard Oppel, "Zur Fugentechnik Bachs" in *Bach-
Jahrbuch* 18 (1921), 9–48 which discusses Bach's uses of *cantus prius facti*. Kurth's *Grundlagen des
linearen Kontrapunkts* (Bern: Max Drechsel, 1917) is of course grounded in a history, including that
of the fugue. In light of our thesis, it is interesting that Hugo Riemann reviews Kurth's argument
as a performance theory in an essay entitled "Die Phrasierung im Lichte einer Lehre von der
Tonvorstellung" in *Zeitschrift für Musikwissenschaft* 1/1 (October, 1918), 26–39. Schenker, although

citing his generation of the subject from the single third-span g–f–e♭. This generation is very involved, however. In citing Marpurg and Marx (while leaving neither unscathed), he immediately dismisses the notion of a purely melodic analysis, arguing that an implicit harmony is always in play within the subject. In his first figure (8a.1) the third-span unfolds to the fifth-divider. Then the leading tone stands in for the fifth-divider (8a.2). In his second figure (8b.1–2) the initial tone of the span is prolonged through an auxiliary a♭, itself supported by the subdominant. Then he again replaces the fifth-divider with the leading tone. In his third figure (8c) the auxiliary acquires its own emulatory third-span (from a♭ through f). In his fourth figure (8d) thirds fill out the inner harmony, and the end of the third-span movement to f is linked to the regained auxiliary a♭ through a slide. In the fifth figure (8e) an upper voice is drawn into the analysis through a simple neighbor motion, the neighbor itself coincident with the place of the fifth-divider. The final figure (8f) details the elaboration of this upper line through a series of rhythmically displaced turns.

Schenker's derivation of the fugue subject would seem quite different in kind from the performance readings encountered earlier. The language that accompanies it is, however, somewhat reminiscent of that which he used to speak of the performance of Mozart's theme.[19] To paraphrase, Schenker speaks of how third-spans compete for the space within which to unfold, the span ranging from g to e♭ being forced to recede by the span bridging a♭ and f, erupting to the surface again only for its most abrupt final descent, and he speaks of how the upper line that circles c is itself compressed – its natural motion in eighth-notes broken, its turns wedged into the spaces between lower-voice attacks.

While Schenker's language is suggestive, there is a curious episode through which this imagery demonstrably links to some notion of

---

he does touch on Kurth, is not interested in the notion of fugue as a historical genre. But then again, he does not elevate Bach as an isolated mathematical master. For a rather fantastic picture of Bach, one which goes beyond the obvious technique to a supposedly hidden technique, and one which Schenker treats (although not at length) in his essay, see Wilhelm Werker, *Studien über die Symmetrie im Bau der Fugen und die motivische Zusammengehörigkeit der Präludien und Fugen des "Wohltemperierten Klaviers" von Johann Sebastian Bach* (Leipzig: Breitkopf und Härtel, 1922). Werker, in common with some of his contemporaries, derives the subject of the C minor fugue from the preceding prelude. He also assigns a structural value to the number twenty-eight, finding, for example, twenty-eight repetitions of the same motive in the prelude which he ties to the twenty-eight attacks of the subject (*Studien über die Symmetrie*, 22–30). His book is also reviewed at length by Arnold Schering, who speaks of Werker's "pseudo-empiricism." See "Kritik: Wilhelm Werker, *Studien über die Symmetrie im Bau der Fugen* ...," *Bach-Jahrbuch* 19 (1922), 72–88.

19 "The Organic in the Fugue," 34–35.

Example 9 A. B. Marx

(a) analysis of the subject of the C minor fugue

(b) tonal answer

(c) continuation of the fugue subject

performance. Quite in character, he takes a recess after his discussion of the subject of the fugue to critique the work of several of his predecessors.[20] As we may recall, Marx and Marpurg had come in earlier for gentle censure. Schenker seems to have been saving himself, or perhaps gathering strength. Here, after his analysis of the subject, he gives free rein to his invective, turning on Riemann, Marx (again), Busoni, and several minor figures. His return to Marx deserves a close reading. He cites a text from Marx's composition treatise wherein is laid out the "kernel" of Bach's fugue subject (Ex. 9a).[21] He then goes on to quote, with qualified approval, Marx's appealing description of the passage:

It is evident that its actual driving force is the descent a♭, g, f, e♭, which emanates from c, first returning to it repeatedly – as if bound to it – and then cutting itself loose.

Schenker's approbation, however, is the smile that precedes the dagger, for he then lets Marx continue, lets Marx speak of the second entry of the subject, lets him drop his guard:

The auxiliary note...g readily introduces this succession, whereas the harmonic note that replaces it in [the answer] – see Ex. 2-410 – would rather descend a second (thus of course completely altering the entire fugal theme), in order to remain consistent and reinforce each important beat with a new harmony.

Schenker here is deceptive. He does not give Marx's ex. 2-410 (Ex. 9b) but immediately introduces Marx's ex. 4-410, wherein Marx gives a reading of the second entrance of the subject which he (Marx) believes preserves the

20 "The Organic in the Fugue," 44.
21 A.B.Marx, *Die Lehre von der musikalischen Komposition, praktisch-theoretisch*, II (Leipzig: Breitkopf und Härtel, 1838; 5th edn. 1864), 536–538. This figure is Marx's 3-410. The translation which follows is taken from *The Masterwork in Music: A Yearbook*, II, p. 44. Marx's descent through a tetrachord is a recurring feature in later analyses of the fugue subject. For example, see Robert Handke, "Diatonik in ihrem Einfluss auf die thematische Gestaltung des Bachschen Fugenbaues" in the *Bach-Jahrbuch* 7 (1910), 1–32. Handke examines linear structures in several of the fugue subjects, and uses the C minor subject to demonstrate a linear motion in the lower portion of the subject, the B minor fugue demonstrating the same at the upper reaches of a subject and the F major demonstrating a linear motion in the middle register ("Diatonik," 12). Beyond this, however, he develops the notion that these linear diatonic motions are balanced or compensated in the fugue. Thus, the descending diatonic lines in the subject and countersubject of the C minor fugue (mm. 1–4) are balanced by a chromatic rise (mm. 5–6): the same behavior recurs at five other points in the fugue ("Diatonik," 12–13). Marx's tetrachord is also the figure that Werker finds to be repeated twenty-eight times in the prelude (*Studien über die Symmetrie*, 22–30). Yeston perceptively notes that this tetrachord, accelerated and situated up a fifth, forms the beginning of the countersubject (*Stratification*, 73).

regularity of harmonic rhythm demonstrated by the first entrance (Ex. 9c).[22] Here Schenker strikes. Marx has committed the unforgivable transgression of presuming to correct – even to rewrite – the master; and moreover his substitution of d for c in the second entrance, the substitution of a "real" for a "tonal" answer, would result in a dissonance against the first voice's e♭. Marx has even missed the connection between the first a♭ and its successor in the fugue subject, and missed completely the structure of interlocking third-spans.

Perhaps we grant Schenker his triumph too casually, however. Indeed, the particular motions with which he dispatches Marx seem somehow deceptive. His argument is less than elegant, his critique of the real answer indecisive (the point he makes about a seventh between e♭ and d carrying no great weight), his turn back to Marx's reading of the subject (of which he had seemed to approve previously) for missing the connection between the two appearances of a♭ puzzling. On reflection, we wonder why he even includes the quotation, and we are bothered by the way in which he interrupts the continuity of thought between Marx's two sentences. Moreover, if we return to the original text we note that not only does Schenker obfuscate Marx's argument, he seems to neglect the fact that Marx makes a case for the real answer not strictly (or even principally) on the basis of theory but rather as a historically valid correction based on a copy of the fugue attributed to a student of Bach and on the reading of an early edition (neither of which, however, is clearly attributed in Marx's text).[23]

Perhaps there is some profit in examining this engagement more closely. Schenker's blustery turn on Marx's real answer may just mask a genuine disquiet. We might note that Marx's "kernel," the even descent from a♭ to e♭ (which he so vividly brings to life in the subject), has, as a conjunct

---

22 Schenker plays games with us here. Marx structures his argument around six examples: ex. 1–410, the fugue subject; ex. 2–410, the soprano entrance of the subject (given in a single line, with the particular c Marx speaks of marked "N.B"); ex. 3–410, the skeleton of the line; ex. 4–410, the continuation of the second entrance of the subject preserving the harmonic rhythm which follows naturally from the substitution of d for the first written c; ex. 5–410, Bach's own continuation in two voices; and ex. 6–410, a figure wherein Marx illustrates how the tonal c implies a static tonic harmony while a real d would imply a dominant (which in turn would prefigure the secondary dominant implied by the first high a). Schenker gives us only ex. 3–410 (of which he does not disapprove) and ex. 4–410 (which he misconstrues and uses to attack Marx).

23 Riemann is not so cavalier. In discussing the second entrance of the subject, he also notes Marx's argument for the real answer, yet he takes the trouble to note Marx's musicological reasoning, and that modern scholarship has cleared up the matter (Analysis, 12). Riemann's own argument for the superiority of the tonal answer (that the modulation to the dominant must be delayed) is weak.

motion binding the passage together, a certain plausibility in Schenker's own terms. We might imagine Schenker feeling compelled to include Marx's reading of the subject (inasmuch as it is close to his own), but we might also imagine him underplaying this quotation and then decisively undercutting Marx's analysis as a whole. In other words, we imagine him misdirecting the reader's attention from that portion of Marx which is dangerous towards that which is vulnerable, thus accomplishing his task not with a quick turn of the wrist but with a sleight of hand.

Going to the question of motive, though, we need ask ourselves why Schenker would find Marx's descending tetrachord dangerous. Perhaps (with a certain sophistication, and adapting Schenker's own language) he finds it dangerous on account of its descent from a♭ to e♭ in the subject, and (by implication) from e♭ to b♭ in the answer, and (by implication again) from a♭ to e♭ in the return of the subject, thus binding the whole of the exposition into a single rather lazy scale, putting forward a rather crude "unity" so at odds with the fecundity of the master. Perhaps, more simply, Schenker feels that Marx's descending tetrachord does not have harmonic implications, or that it implies a reading of the subject which does not, in fact, necessarily entail a harmony.

Of course, on this last point, Schenker himself has conceded to Marx that the subject must be read harmonically, and in actuality Marx's entire argument for the real answer is based on harmonic considerations. In fact, it is this harmonic argument which Schenker evades by having Marx putatively "rewrite" Bach. Indeed, we discover the source of Schenker's unease in Marx's own words (words which Schenker feels compelled to quote). As we recall, Marx uses the phrase "to remain consistent and reinforce each important beat with a new harmony." Marx's descending tetrachord strongly marks the surface meter: this is why he feels compelled to put forward a real answer which similarly marks the surface meter through its harmonic rhythms. Schenker's nested third-spans, by contrast, while they may translate onto a rigidly metric surface, unfold in a space remarkable by being not so marked.

Herein lies the genius of his reading. Schenker seems to have looked for an underlying structure which resists the mechanical regularity of the surface of Bach's passage. Herein can also be found the point of contact between Schenker's derivation and the later nineteenth- and early twentieth-century performance editions. As we recall, the assorted editors of the performance reading attempt (to an increasing degree) to shape the passage in terms of an interpretive dynamic that, if it does not suppress the mechanistic surface of the passage, does indeed attempt to give nuance to this surface. With the exception of Riemann in his first reading, each in his way seems to feel that the a♭ in the second measure of the subject has a certain importance in this regard, yet none is able to arrive at a reading that makes sense of this attack. Schenker, by contrast, looks to the interior of the passage, to the space within which the third-spans are locked in their metaphorical struggle, and therein locates a dynamic that actively contradicts the metric rigidity of the surface, a resistance that erupts to the surface in the second a♭. Riemann gives sweep to the passage by positing a macrorhythm or hypermeasure with a secondary stress on the opening of the second measure and the primary stress on the opening of the third measure. Schenker sees the passage as a sort of crystallized trajectory. The g that opens his principal third-span is first heard as a consonance, next (as the passing auxiliary to the auxiliary a♭) as the most dissonant pitch in the line (supported by e♭ and c over the bass f), and after almost vanishing, in its third sounding, settles in as the initiation of an escape motion over the fifth-divider.

It could even be ventured that this derivation entails a sort of performance, one Schenker would claim to be more complex and nuanced than that specified by any of the editors. We would assume a correlation between dynamics and stress and the positioning of particular events within the derivation, those events occurring earlier in the derivation being downplayed, in comparison, by those which occur later.[24] This performance would bring out the turns around the upper c with particular stress on each initial attack (because of the compression of the figure). The concluding high d, further back in the derivation, would be treated with care, perhaps released gently before the subsequent attack. The initial g of the inner voice is, of course, recessive, played down. The a♭ which follows would carry more weight but would, in turn, play to the dissonant, unsupported foreground g before falling off slightly to f. The regained a♭, standing as the release of the span initiated by the first a♭, could be played just under its predecessor (and not over-weighted compared to the preceding f) before the passage recedes dramatically into the background with the fall from g to e♭.

---

24 In other words, I propose a simple mechanization of Schenker's own view. We read (significantly enough): "This, of course, does not mean that the tones of the fundamental line need be overemphasized, as are the entrances in a poor performance of a fugue. The player who is aware of the coherence of a work will find interpretative means which allow the coherence to be heard." (*Free Composition*, 8). See also the section entitled "Urlinie and Performance" of the "Further Considerations of the Urlinie I" in *The Masterwork in Music*, I, 109–110.

In fact, in examining the working sketch for the entire fugue and in comparing it with Bartók's performance edition, we can practically imagine Schenker, the pianist, coaching a student (Ex. 10a–b).[25] Again, as a simple, commonsense rule of thumb, we assume the notion that events farther back in the derivation need stand (as it were) in the shadows. In other words, a truly vivid performance would allow the background events to fend for themselves and bring out the inventive surface of the music. We imagine a performance of the subject focused on the work around the upper c (the closest event to the surface), and further imagine an emphasis on, then an abrupt fall from, the regained c in m. 3. The countersubject, reoccupying that same inner register, would likewise come to the fore in mm. 3–4, deflecting attention from the structural g in the soprano that binds the passage together. The structural f in the soprano that closes m. 6 would not be stressed (contrary to Bartók's reading), nor would the succeeding soprano e♭. For this reason, the reentrance of the subject in m. 7 would be brought out and the fall from e♭ would build to the inner f. The left hand's run in mm. 9–11 would be brought out (at the expense of the right hand). In particular, this run would be pushed through to its close on a♭ in order to defuse the soprano's arrival at a structural e♭ in m. 11. As in Bartók's reading, the right hand would be let loose in its corresponding run – mm. 12–15 – and the energy acquired at the highest c would be allowed to bolster the succeeding restatement of the fugue subject. The structural d in the soprano of m. 17 would thus emerge almost as an overtone of the cadential sonority. Likewise, the initiation of the final octave descent on the soprano c of m. 20 would also have to "come out of" the momentum of the previous two measures, and the reinitiation of the fugue subject would have to play to its close on f. As in the corresponding episode in mm. 9–11, the episode in mm. 22–25 would bring out the bravura left hand at the expense of the octave descent in the right hand. The fifth descent in the inner register of mm. 27–29 could be emphasized so as to make the true conclusion of the octave-span in m. 29 sound like a compression of the previous move. The slight decelerando which Bartók places in m. 29 should perhaps be better placed, or at least anticipated, in m. 28.

We might even go so far as to imagine Schenker specifying certain heuristic guidelines for the performance of the fugue. He might ask that

25 Ex. 10a is given in the original text as "Urlinie-Tafel zu Seite 59", (appended to Jahrbuch II). Ex. 10b is from *Das wohltemperierte Klavier* I, ed. Béla Bartók (Budapest: Zenemükiadó Vállalat, 1967), 30–31.

Example 10

(a) Heinrich Schenker's Urlinie-Tafel, of Bach's C minor fugue

Example 10 (*cont.*)
(b) Béla Bartók's edition of the fugue

FUGA

a 3 voci

Z. 4475

Example 10 (*cont.*)
(b) Béla Bartók's edition of the fugue (*cont.*)

long strings of running notes be brought out, for example, or that individual sonorities or passages be weighted towards or centered in the inner registers rather than in the extreme registers. We need not go so far as to imagine Schenker specifying a strict translation protocol, however. We certainly could not imagine him using his analysis as the basis for a performance edition.

We might be tempted, pursuing this line, to distinguish Schenker's structures (and their relation to execution) from the notational emendations of (again) Riemann's performance theory according to the presence of an organized body of interpretive rules, the former lacking and the latter embodying such a protocol. Yet such a distinction does not hold up under scrutiny. In looking to the sorts of performance directions entailed by Schenker's reading, we note that they involve nuances of dynamics, shading, registration, and tempo.[26] But we also note that these are exactly the sorts of nuances that Riemann grants to the discretion of the performer: the phrase slur is not in itself an articulatory marking but an abstract dynamic guideline, a description of tensions and releases; not an executory direction but a conceptual indication. Thus, in speaking of performance we cannot

---

26 For an example of the sort of language Schenker uses when speaking of performance, I quote from his essay "Chopin: Etude in E♭ Minor, Op. 10, Nr. 6," trans. Ian Bent in *The Masterwork in Music: A Yearbook*, I: 81–89; quotation p. 88:

Now to performance. The manuscript gives no metronome marking; Chopin cannot have determined it until later. The sense of reaching forward towards the $\hat{3}$ of bars 3–4, and towards the IV and II of bars 5 and 7, gives a clear idea of the tempo: however much one may come to terms with localized diminution motives from one bar to the next, the sense of striving towards those other goals must also be communicated in performance. The semiquaver figure is played *legatissimo*, the fingers literally tripping over one another in an effort to allow the neighbor-note motive b♭–a–b♭ in bar 1, c♭¹–b♭–c♭¹ in bar 2 etc. to come through. The *forte* in bar 5 should be played as no more than a momentarily louder surge; it applies only to the upward transfer of the diminution launched by the e♭².

Bars 16–40 cannot be interpreted correctly without a keen awareness of their internal cohesive forces. Above all, the performer should be at pains not to treat the b♮¹ of bar 21 as the beginning of a new section (see above). Bars 21–4, which provide the space for the c♭² to expand, may appear to flow along ever more peacefully; but the first indication of a restlessness that is to come – conveyed by Chopin's hairpin *crescendo* marking in bar 24 (a stroke of genius!) – counteracts this, strategically placed as it is to deter the player from any temptation to introduce a caesura at this point. Immediately, bars 25–6 and 27–8 come out as self-contained units by virtue of the hairpin *crescendo* and *decrescendo* markings, and this betokens a growing turbulence of which the *stretto e cresc.* in bar 30 marks the final thrust. However, from bar 33 onwards the performer should observe the slurs that Chopin has placed over each pair of bars; only by so doing will he be able to gauge the right degree of accent for the g♮¹ and g♭¹ of bars 38 and 39. The c♯² in bar 49 must be taken softly, and the initial semiquavers in the right hand of bar 50 should be allowed to glide by as passing notes between b♭♭¹ and f♭¹ (a♮¹ and f♭¹ in Chopin's notation – see the Foreground Graph).

Example 11   Heinrich Schenker, Appendix V, *Jahrbuch* II

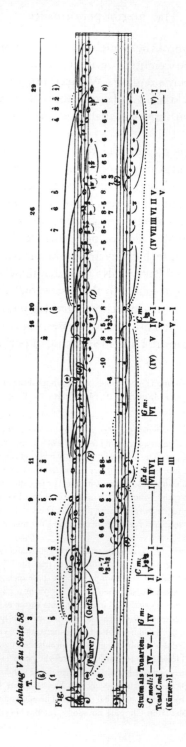

separate in kind Schenker's analysis from Riemann's performance reading. Both determine what we might think of as the inflection of the musical passage.

In fact, we may equate Schenker's analysis with Riemann's performance theory yet more tellingly. Returning to Schenker's reading of the fugue subject, we recall the pride with which he claims an analytic parsimony for his derivation of the passage from a single third-span. We recall being puzzled by the contradiction between this claim and the obvious complexity of the derivation, and we recall accounting for Schenker's choice of the third-span as a primitive (rather than Marx's tetrachord) by noting that the third-span does not simply provide an explanatory efficacy but also stands as a sort of dynamic which resists the surface metric, hence inflecting the passage. We might now read this third-span as something more than a pitch structure, something more than a musical fragment. If we are to make the point (along with Schenker) that the fugue subject itself (i.e. as originally notated) entails a performance, we cannot but grant (or grant implicitly) the same capacity to the third-span. We might think of it as a representation of a single motion. Since Schenker always groups it under a slur, we might think of it in terms of the phrase slur, as a single breath with an attack, a swell, and a release. We might even venture so far as to say that Schenker does not so much reject Riemann's theoretical construct as disentangle it from the mechanics of editing and move it from outside of to inside the text. In other words, let us say that Schenker denies the phrase slur out of the conviction that it is already (although in a different form) present.

Such an internal phrase slur is at once less and more complex than its external counterpart. It does not require a metric framework or a theorization of meter. Indeed, as we have noted, it may use surface meter as a foil. Yet at the same time we cannot but feel that Schenker intends a far more subtle inflection of the musical surface than that put forward by Riemann's relatively simple succession of dynamic groupings. In fact, Schenker models such a subtlety by locating within the music a complex of such dynamic groupings. On examining his final sketch of the fugue (Ex. 11), we might say that he extrapolates from the interaction of the first fugue and the subject a whole series of layered inflections.[27] We can

---

27 This sketch is given in the original as "Anhang V zu Seite 58". In support of my argument I would direct the reader to a passage which speaks of performance in Schenker's "The Largo of Bach's Sonata No. 3 for Solo Violin", trans. John Rothgeb in *The Masterwork in Music: A Yearbook*, I, 31–38; see pp. 37–38 in particular. He writes: "Once the content of the piece is completely understood, performance poses no problems. In my forthcoming treatise, 'The Art of Performance,' it will be

Example 12

translate these groupings as "performances" (Ex. 12). The conventions of this translation are simple. We first delete the contrapuntal support, then fix the pitches of Schenker's spans as attack points, and finally assign a dynamic shape (a swell on the attack pitch, a diminuendo on the release pitches which are without exception displaced to the end of the span) to each span. These groupings of course encompass octave-spans, fifth-spans, third-spans, extensions and the like, yet we may simply presume any structure held under a slur to conform to the same shaping.[28]

We discover that one stratum seems to contradict the next. To choose the most obvious example, the conclusion of the attack of the broadest span in m. 9 coincides with the release of yet another span; likewise the release of the first span coincides with the attack of another span. Yet on reflection, we should not speak of contradiction but of modulation (in the physical rather than the musical sense of the term): the dynamic complexity Schenker hears in the fugue is a composite, a product of the successively more subtle inflection or modulation of a simple dynamic motion.

In moving Riemann's phrase slur from the outside to the inside of the text, in defining its function not as a convention but as a theoretic entity, Schenker is thus able to transform what can at times be a rather brutally mechanical construction into something both supple and powerful. He instructs us that the composer's voice is not a thing to be recaptured through the agency of an editorial apparatus, but rather something that has been present all along (if we were but to listen), that the true performance

systematically shown for the first time that dynamics, like voice-leading and diminution, are organized according to structural levels, genealogically, as it were. For each level of voice-leading, whether background or foreground, and for each level of diminution, there is a corresponding dynamic level of the first order, second order, and so forth." Schenker then has the reader note two sets of dynamic markings which are part of a background–foreground sketch of the Largo and goes on to explicate how these implied dynamics are to be realized in performance. Interestingly enough, this essay follows immediately on "The Art of Improvisation" and "Abolish the Phrasing Slur," and is itself followed by the essay "The Prelude of Bach's Partita No. 3 for Solo Violin" which contains a similar sketch annotated with dynamic markings. To the best of my knowledge, Schenker does not provide the same sort of sketch for any other texts: perhaps this has something to do with the fact that these are pieces for solo violin, the technical issues of which are perhaps somewhat beyond Schenker (although he has dealt with some notational issues in "Abolish the Phrasing Slur").

28 Schenker argues against any notion that octave, fifth, and third descents are different in kind. The consonance–dissonance–consonance structure which underlies each derives from the retention of the initiating tone until the penultimate tone: indeed, the "tension-span" is ultimately always reducible to the simple stepwise passing motion characteristic of the upper voice. See the section entitled "The Primary Note of the Linear Progression" in the "Further Consideration of the Urlinie" in *The Masterwork in Music* II, 3–5.

is not one which recovers a lost sensibility but rather one which allows the interior performance (or ensemble of performances) to sing through.[29]

THE PALEOGRAPHIC ARGUMENT

If we conceive Schenker's analysis in terms of an interior performance (or a composite of performances) we gain a certain purchase on rather strong claims he is to later make with regards to performance practice. We might even venture that Schenker, with the incorporation of conventions of performance into his analysis, merges the domains of music theory and musical interpretation previously brought into proximity by Riemann. But if we recall the original purposes of this investigation, we might instead use this notion of interior performances to sponsor a theoretical reconstruction of the way in which (immediately) the conception of an improvisatory imagination and (remotely) the reading of the history of music come to structure the late analysis of *Free Composition*.

We will remember that *Ornamentation* and (somewhat differently) the essay on the phrase slur argue vigorously for the original text (in *Ornamentation* against an indisputably flagrant example of editorial emendation and alteration, and in the essay against a general practice). Schenker makes his case historically in the first work, theoretically in the second. In neither does he acknowledge any debt to the work of contemporary musicologists. This, perhaps, should not come as any surprise given the particular domain of later nineteenth-century historical musicology, concerned as it is, most broadly, with the recovery of musics standing outside of the canon, and most particularly with the mechanics of musical transcription and textural criticism. From our own vantage point, however, such a debt appears more than plausible. (We might even see in Schenker's polemic some reflection of the current disagreements over historically authentic performance.) In fact, to make a counter-intuitive move, we would initially venture that Schenker's rejection of editorial intervention in *Ornamentation*, his rejection of the editorial phrase slur, and even his elucidation of the performance of Mozart's passage are all indebted to the discipline of musical paleography, to the decoding of early notation which,

---

29 We read: "A performance, in serving background, middleground, and foreground, can employ the greatest variety of color. Even the richest and most varied resources of performance can be taught – and learned – with great exactness. On the other hand, commitment to background, middleground, and foreground excludes all arbitrary personal interpretation" (*Free Composition*, xxiii).

through the work of a number of pioneering figures, had come to form the cornerstone of historical and comparative musicology.[30]

To make our case, we first present a complex of four overlapping arguments – arguments about the nature, efficiency, consistency, and economies of notation that lie at the epistemological foundations of musical paleography.[31]

The paleographer first argues that musical notation is to be taken as something opaque, that the evidence of musical notation is confined strictly to that which is visible, to the mark on the page. In other words, the paleographer must proceed not from the simple assumption that a notation is a way of encoding a familiar musical sensibility but rather from the less intuitive assumption that a notation constitutes the representation of a musical sensibility which is in some fundamental way alien. Speaking epistemologically, this argument gives paleography some standing as an empirical discipline. Speaking pragmatically, it functions in large part as a caution. While the medievalist, for example, believes transcription to be possible when (as is the case with a-diastematic chant notations) one can assume a continuity between early and later sources, or when (as with

30 A majority of the music historians of the later nineteenth century have understood paleography as a discipline adjunct to the narrative project of defining and describing the periodic evolution of music, and much of the musical research of the time concerned itself with the music of the seventeenth through nineteenth centuries wherein paleography did not come into play. Yet I would argue that it is the discipline of paleography which definitively establishes (in concert with the work of the psychoacousticians) music as a scientific study, as a musicology. Such texts as the pioneering *Paléographie Musicale*, ed. André Mocquereau and J. Gajard (Solesmes et Tournai, 1889–), Gustav Jacobsthal's *Die Mensuralnotenschrift des 12. und 13. Jahrhunderts* (Berlin: J. Springer, 1871), and Riemann's *Studien zur Geschichte der Notenschrift* (Leipzig: Breitkopf und Härtel, 1878) stand as a sort of cutting edge for the new science. Schenker devotes a lengthy footnote in *Harmony* to critical editions of old music, and as we would expect, he is hostile to the uncritical resurrection of historic music predating his canon and to the musicologist's enterprise in general (p. 69). Yet it is significant that he is familiar with this project, and that he gives such length and energy to his critique. He is himself obviously not immune to the "scientific" authority of the musicological method.

31 This expansion of the ramifications of paleography is my own. Katherine Bergeron, in her work on the politics of the Solesmes edition of the chant, has brought to light the ideologies buried within the paleographic project, showing how the Vatican supported this work as a cooption of the historical sciences and how with the completion of a new Graduale the church hierarchy abandoned the project. See Katherine Bergeron, Representation, Reproduction, and the Revival of Gregorian Chant at Solesmes (Ph.D. dissertation, Cornell University, 1989). Yet while the methodologies of the human sciences could be, and often were, suborned for overt political ends, and while the nineteenth-century turn to medieval music carried complex political baggage, I would argue that epistemologically powerful methodologies such as that of musical paleography were destined to transcend their motivation, coming not to subordinate the unfamiliar to a familiar agenda but actually to create a consciousness of difference.

fourteenth-century polyphony) one is in possession of contemporary theoretic sources, he or she must still regard transcription in general as problematic, must still assume that any transcription is in some way distorted.

The paleographer next argues that a system of notation is, by definition, internally coherent. Lacking grounds with which to make any judgment, one must assume that a notation is not in any way arbitrary or inconsistent and assume that no symbol or class of symbols can be taken to have greater or lesser importance than any other symbol or class of symbols. The task of paleography is to establish the laws that govern the internal economy of the particular system of notation as a whole.

The paleographer must then argue that a particular system of notation constitutes the most efficient representation of its particular musical sensibility. One may draw links between different notational systems, as when one assumes that a-diastematic and diastematic sources (i.e. earlier sources which give only unstaffed neumes and later sources which give exact pitch information) of the same chant share pitch content to some degree, yet one cannot assume that any notational system is an incomplete or inferior version of another: notation does not perfect itself but rather evolves to meet changing musical concerns.

Lastly, the paleographer needs to argue that a notational system maps a general economy of musical production. In other words, a notational system gives evidence not simply of pitch or rhythm but of a totality (if not a completely reconstructable totality) of how and why music is made, of compositional process and performance practice. Thus, for example, the disposition of a polyphony by part rather than by score would indicate a process of successive composition of lines. (Thus also, to turn the tables, the notational innovations of the nineteenth-century performing edition give insight into the increasing distinction between the respective tasks of the professional composer and the performer, and the rise of the authoritative mediator.)

At first we might miss the relevance of this matrix to Schenker's own program. The work of the paleographer seems far afield from that of Schenker: while he is conversant with the general outlines of medieval music, we see no evidence of an interest in notations and sources and the like. Yet in his championship of the autographs of specific pieces, and particularly in his argument for the original text, we see the matrix of paleographic arguments turned not on an alien system of notation but on the notation of the masters. This move is most dramatically illustrated in his essay attacking the phrase slur. Considering the first three of these points (while holding the fourth in reserve), Schenker argues against the assumption that the historically remote composer and the contemporary performer share a common musical sensibility that can be theoretically isolated (implicit in the conception of the phrase slur). In simple terms, Schenker argues that the notation of the masters must be taken as the sole indication of the meaning, as such, of the music. He likewise argues the consistency and efficiency of the master's notation. We remember that he does not treat Mozart's notation of the accented passing tones as an outdated convention but rather takes this notation as the direct means of conveying a particular affect.

We find yet a different subtext beneath the phrase slur essay. As noted, the ultimate target of Schenker's polemic (in the essay) is Hugo Riemann's principles of editing, though he never acknowledges Riemann by name. Specifically, he never acknowledges the systematic or psychological claims put forward for the phrase slur, if even to retreat to some vague bromide about performance being an art rather than a science. Yet as we see, he covertly sets the scientific discipline of the paleographer against the psychological science of the phrase slur. He fixes, systematically, the text as a historical document. Moreover, he smuggles a delicate and abstract notion of the history of music into his analysis. We might again turn to Riemann as a foil. There is, indeed, a particular irony here. Where Schenker gives little attention throughout his writings to such things as biographical or archival research, Riemann, throughout his career, concerns himself with the substance and methodology of historical musicology. He is also concerned with defining the respective domains of his various theoretical and historical projects and establishing points of engagement. The mechanics of performance editing is one such point of engagement. As the unattributed editor renders Mozart's theme into what he believes to be a more accurate or more musical notation through the use of the phrase slur, so Riemann does in his transcriptions of such diverse works as those of Bach, Josquin, and Machaut, and even in his transcriptions of the corpus of plainchant. In his attempt to make such lost or marginalized bodies of music "sing" to the contemporary audience, he steps beyond paleographic skepticism and subsumes all music in a single universal sensibility.[32]

---

32 The best introduction to Riemann's recuperation of old music is the anthology of transcriptions entitled *Musikgeschichte in Beispielen*, 3 vols. (Leipzig: Breitkopf und Härtel, 1911–12). His reading of old music, even by his own terms, is not without problems. The phrase slur cannot come into

Hence, under Riemann's scrutiny, the historical quality of the work is defined (or perhaps confined) by the circumstance or situation of its production, by its style, by the appearance of the notation in which it is given to the modern editor. Yet however much the work is musical, it seems to stand outside of the history of music.

Schenker's concern with original notation, by contrast, locates the historical presence of the text within the concrete manifestation of the text itself (though he does restrict this application to a very narrow class of works). In other words, neither the circumstance nor the situation of a text (as determined by external evidence) gives it a place in the history of music; not the style, but its unique and intrinsic dynamic.

THE PHILOLOGICAL PARADIGM

The analysis of the musical text thus itself cannot stand strictly outside of history. This is not to suggest the obviously contrafactual notion that Schenker comes to hold to some historically sensitive analysis (although his concern with C. P. E. Bach's writings on music intimates a limited acceptance of historical theory), but rather to suggest that in constructing his analysis, he appeals, however covertly and strangely, to a second great historical science of the nineteenth century, the science of philology.

To briefly sketch an outline of this science, we recall that the comparative linguists of the early nineteenth century develop a methodology for empirically investigating the production of language as a historical phenomenon.[33] Their most original insight holds that the history of language

---

play for the unevenly melismatic vocal lines of the Middle Ages (although it does return with the syllabic lines of the early seventeenth century). Untexted lines are another matter. A particularly curious reading of Baude Cordier's "Tout par compass" is given in the *Handbuch der Musikgeschichte* I/2 (Leipzig: Breitkopf und Härtel, 1905), 352. Another interesting example is his transcription of Dunstable's "Veni creator spiritus" in *Handbuch der Musikgeschichte* II/1 (Leipzig: Breitkopf und Härtel, 1907), foldout after 114. The difficulties he encounters in applying his metric analysis to older music are best illustrated by his transcription of a Willaert *Ricercare* in the same volume (*Handbuch* II/1, 450–451). One gets the sense that for Riemann the history of performance parallels the history of theory: both involve a process of clarification. We might also draw a parallel here with the reconstructions of historic instruments early in the twentieth century, reconstructions which to our ears seem more gauged to modern timbral preference than concerned with authenticity.

33 We speak here of what the later nineteenth century would term comparative philology (as opposed to the traditional classical philology which occupied itself with the exegesis of Greek and Latin texts). Michel Foucault makes a very strong case for the importance of philology in the formation of modern thought (an importance he thinks has been previously overlooked: the discussion herein is loosely indebted in its entirety to his ideas) in *Les Mots et les choses* (Paris: Editions Gallimard, 1966),

is to be found internally, and that this history can be established by bracketing out the meaning of language (the central concern of eighteenth-century comparative grammar and of classical philology) and looking instead to grammar and phonetics. (In other words, while etymology remains of interest, grammar and phonetics, as more stable constituents of language, are taken as surer markers of a language's derivation.) For example (to take the benchmark of modern philology) a comparison of such languages as classical Greek, Latin, Sanskrit, and

trans. (unattributed) as *The Order of Things* (London:Tavistock, 1970; NewYork:Vantage, 1973).All citations hereafter are to theVantage edition.The language he uses to explain this neglect is typically seductive:"in short, the whole body of philological work accomplished by Grimm, Schlegel, Rask, and Bopp, has remained on the fringes of our historical awareness, as though it had merely provided the basis for a somewhat lateral and esoteric discipline – as though, in fact, it was not the whole mode of being of language (and of our own language) that had been modified through it. Certainly we ought not to attempt a justification of this neglect in spite of the importance of this change, but, on the contrary, on the basis of its importance, and on that of the blind proximity that the event still preserves for our eyes, in their continuing attachment to their customary lights. The fact is that, even at the time when it occurred, this event was already enveloped, if not in secret, at least in a certain discretion" (*The Order of Things*, 281). He likewise makes the point that it is necessary for Franz Bopp, in the seminal *Vergleichende Grammatik des Sanskrit, Zend, Armenischen, Griechischen, Lateinischen, Litthauischen, Altslawischen, Gothischen und Deutschen* [1833–1852] 3rd edn. (Berlin: F. Dümmler, 1868–1871), to ignore the external history of language in order to arrive at an internal history, to ignore the historical placement of Sanskrit, Classical Greek, Latin, and modern European languages in order to discover how their inflections array themselves temporally (*The Order of Things*, 280–294).We should note that Bopp does not take phonetics into account in his picture. Interestingly enough, comparative philology itself undergoes a sort of revolution in the 1870s, when, among other things, philologists grasp the laws of phonetic change and Sanskrit loses its romantic status as the oldest of the extant Indo-Euopean languages. The standard history of comparative philology is found in Holger Pedersen, *The Discovery of Language; Linguistic Science in the Nineteenth Century*, trans. John Spargo (Bloomington: Indiana University Press, 1962). The comparative method acquired an almost mystical prestige in the later nineteenth century, particularly in certain circles in France.We note that the decisive move in the creation of modern linguistics can be attributed to Saussure, who separated philology from grammatics, laying the foundation for structural grammar and phonology. In Germany, August Böckh's posthumous *Encyklopädie und Methodologie der philologischen Wissenschaften*, ed. Ernst Bratuscheck (Leipzig: B. G. Teubner, 1877) was quite influential. Böckh is known primarily as a classical philologist, yet he makes a place for grammatic philology in his system. Interestingly enough he presents philology as the basis for all of the human sciences (in so far as language has priority), and argues for a hermeneutics grounded in the philologically revealed historical presence. He also draws a distinction between interpretation and criticism, the first being directed towards the object itself, the second toward the object's relations with other objects. See the introduction to Kurt Mueller-Vollmer, ed., *The Hermeneutics Reader* (New York: Continuum, 1985), 20–23. Pierre Aubry and Johann Beck, two musicologists notorious for preparing to fight a duel over precedence in the application of theories of modal rhythm to Medieval secular monophony, were both trained in comparative philology. (Aubry gave his life for musicology in a fencing accident as he prepared.) We should note that philology is both historically and theoretically anterior to paleography.

the modern European languages reveals a number of resemblances of vocabulary. Yet these languages most clearly coincide not in their vocabularies but in their systems of verbal inflection, and thus it is in the comparison of these inflectional systems that a family of languages can be delineated and a common ancestry (Indo-European) established. The philologist can, through a generalization of the laws of phonetic change, fix an internal chronology, a family tree for this grouping of languages. (Sanskrit is determined to be the eldest of the surviving Indo-European languages.)

To draw this rather esoteric discipline, however briefly, into our discussion may seem arbitrary. On reflection, though, we would do well not to underestimate the power of comparative philology as a methodological paradigm. A philological paradigm underlies much of what comes into being in the later nineteenth century as the new science of musicology. Most obviously, it authorizes the discipline of textual criticism wherein the mechanics of scribal practice, as evidenced by scribal error, common variants and the comparison of specific repertoires of various manuscripts, and evaluated by such general laws as *difficilior lectio potior* (which holds that the more complex version of a figure or passage is earlier), enables the musicologist to construct a *stemma* demonstrating the transmission of a piece or a repertoire, and even (in principle) enables the musicologist to reconstruct lost stages in this transmission and give some idea of the earliest textual reading.[34] Less obviously, the philological paradigm allows the musicologist to define empirically internal families of texts within single manuscripts and array these families in historical strata.[35] Indirectly, we

34 Textual criticism, deriving from the work of Karl Lachmann early in the nineteenth century, represents in some way a reconciliation of classical and comparative philologies (or the application of comparative methods to the reconstruction of the classical text). Inasmuch as many pieces of Medieval music exist in a number of manuscript copies, and hence can be examined in terms of scribal practice (such as common variants, scribal errors and the like), Lachmann's discipline translates easily into the domain of musical studies. The standard modern guide to this subject is Paul Maas, *Textual Criticism*, trans. Barbara Flower (Oxford: Clarendon Press, 1958).

35 For example, the repertoire of twelfth- and early thirteenth-century Parisian polyphony is contained in three complex thirteenth-century manuscripts. The practice of Notre Dame polyphony (the creation of the *Magnus Liber* by Léonin, the innovations of Pérotin) is reported in a fourth theoretic source. The first (and still essential) systematic examination of these manuscripts is found in Friedrich Ludwig's *Repertorium organorum recentioris et motetorum vetustissimi stili*, Part I (Halle: Niemeyer, 1910). Ludwig takes the initial steps toward disentangling the different strata of these manuscripts and toward the reconstruction of the *Magnus Liber*, and his work remains central to more recent attempts to arrive at a compositional history of the Notre Dame school. Also, it has been known since the later nineteenth century that the suppression of earlier chant traditions by the Carolingian recension was (at least at its earlier statements) incomplete, and that traces of (in particular) Gallican chant survive in several of the earliest Graduals. The first consideration given

would even see the philological paradigm reaching outside of the domain of medieval music to create the various musical discourses of genre, influence, compositional process and thematic borrowing – all of which posit distinctions of musical dialect which, in turn, reveal historical networks. To speak of a body of work contemporary with that of Schenker, we might locate the most systematic attempt to establish a neo-philological historiography of music in Guido Adler's proposal for a comprehensive style criticism. (Adler would use something approaching the comparative method when he speaks of gauging coincidence and contrast amongst distinct musical languages defined by specific stylistic norms.)[36]

Again, though, it might be objected that none of these investigations is demonstrably and directly indebted to the comparative philology of the linguists. In none of these cases is music truly treated as a philologically available language (or are musics treated as philologically available languages).[37] Perhaps the notion of comparative stylistics comes closest to this

to these survivals is found in Peter Wagner's *Einführung in die Gregorianischen Melodien* (Leipzig: Breitkopf und Härtel, 1911–21). Wagner's work, like that of Ludwig, gives rise to an impressive body of later scholarship.

36 Guido Adler's program for a comprehensive style-criticism is put forward in *Der Stil in der Musik*, Book 1 (Leipzig: Breitkopf und Härtel, 1911) and in his *Methode der Musikgeschichte* (Leipzig: Breitkopf und Härtel, 1919). For a brief synopsis of his program see "Style-Criticism," trans. Oliver Strunk in *Musical Quarterly* 20 (1934), 172–176. Adler's agenda is important in that it typifies a new conception of "style" as a musically autonomous and definable quality of the particular piece or composer. Style is taken as a grammatic rather than semantic attribute. The identification of Adler's program with philological presuppositions made in this argument is admittedly open to question. Adler himself affiliates his program with Woelfflin's conception of art-historical style, Yet we might be inclined to read his agenda in terms of the contemporary attempt to establish Comparative Literature (and hence the broad application of the comparative method) as an independent discipline in the university, a struggle which at times involves identifying this project both with and against the already established disciplines of Classical and Germanic philology. I would not directly attribute to Adler any intention to reconstruct a stemmatic history through the application of the comparative method, yet one of the marks of his agenda is the rejection of any broad periodic scheme for music history derived from other disciplines. A slightly earlier formulation of a systematic stylistics is found in Hugo Riemann's *Kleines Handbuch der Musikgeschichte mit Periodisierung nach Stilprinzipien und Formen* (Leipzig: Breitkopf und Härtel, 1908). A modern attempt at an objective or statistical stylistics is found in Jan LaRue, *Guidelines for Style Analysis* (New York: W. W. Norton, 1970).

37 For these reasons, perhaps the most convincing application of the method of comparative philology to musical groupings is the attempt on the part of several central European ethnomusicologists – or, by the German usage, "comparative musicologists" – to discover ancestral musical languages in the modern oral traditions of Hungary, Romania, and Bulgaria. See Béla Bartók, *The Hungarian Folksong*, ed. Benjamin Suchoff, trans. M. D. Calvocoressi (Albany: State University of New York, 1981), 1–11, and Zoltán Kodály, "The Primitive Stratum in Hungarian Folk Music" in *Folk Music of Hungary*, trans. R. Tempest and C. Jolly (New York: Praeger, 1971), 23–61. Both Bartók and Kodály

ideal. Yet such a stylistics (or the conception of a musical problem in terms of such a stylistics) seems beyond reach. Let us say we were to examine mid-eighteenth-century instrumental music linguistically. First we would have to define what would constitute a language in our system. Would a language be determined by composer, by nationality, by genre or form, or by some other criterion? Next we would have to define a basis for comparison and we would encounter similar problems. Ultimately, we would have to ask ourselves what purpose is to be served by such a project: is it intended to yield a sort of idealized history against which to gauge the actual history of music or is it intended to yield various groupings or families of mid-eighteenth-century musical languages?

There appear to be numerous pragmatic considerations impeding any direct appropriation of the philological method to musical studies. On very few occasions in musicology can one even posit (let alone establish) a distinct historical origin for a collection of phenomena. One can speak of the original reading of a piece, yet one cannot so easily speak of an original style and its intervening stages of development. Musical texts seem most conveniently to group themselves in networks rather than in family trees. Any development of a notion of style tends to be captured by the task of defining the relationship between the individual text and a general norm, tends to become bogged down when speaking of ideal types or parametric measurement. Indeed, the specification of distinct authorship within an exclusively written mode of transmission cannot but render any treatment of music as a language suspect.

recognize "old" and "new" strata of Hungarian folksong. The former is distinguished from neighboring Romanian, Croatian, and Slovak folksong by its pentatonicism and predilection for the fifth transposition, and related to the folksong of the Chuvash and Cheremis peoples of the Volga region. A potentially quite interesting project is advanced in Alan Lomax's *Folk Song Style and Culture* (Washington D.C.: American Association for the Advancement of Science, Publication No. 88, 1968). Lomax's stylistics is based on vocal performance, grading musics from around the world on such qualities as solo versus ensemble preference, tonal and rhythmic blend, ratio of words to pitches, melodic shape, phrase length, range, embellishment, tempo, rubato, glissandi, tremolo, register, nasality, and raspiness. Through the comparison of performances, he arrives at six principal musical languages and three isolates: the principal languages comprising North American, South American, Insular Pacific, African (sub-Saharan), European, and Old High Culture (Mediterranean, Islamic, Turkic and Indian, East Asian), and the isolates comprising Australian, Arctic Asian, and Tribal Indian. He examines each of these languages in turn for homogeneity, sub-dialects, and degree of similarity to other languages. Lomax conceives his project sociologically, as a way of relating music with culture. (For example, he finds a direct correlation between vocal tension and sexual mores.) Yet inasmuch as he arrives at a "grammatic" or "phonological" description of performance, it is possible to imagine that his analysis might reveal some deep historical links between musics.

There are more fundamental methodological impediments to such an appropriation – two in particular of interest. First, if we are to conceive, as we have, the comparative study of a particular repertoire such as mid-eighteenth-century instrumental music, it requires us to step outside of history, outside of the world of historiographically available evidence or – more accurately – to take a slice out of this evidence and examine it in isolation. Second, we need remember that the critical insight which allowed for the creation of comparative philology involved a shift in focus from the content or meaning of language, from the root, as it were, to the grammatical form of language, to the inflection of the verb. This is where constructions such as style, genre, thematic structure, or form are suggestive. We might conceive them as grammatical functions of the musical text as opposed to some intrinsic semantic quality of the text. But this conception is problematic. These constructs have their roots in the notions of affect, rhetorical disposition, and manner which were central to the eighteenth century's nominological definition of musical meaning.[38] Yet while we may find this derivation problematic, it would seem to hold inasmuch as it is perhaps empirically impossible to define qualities of music that lie outside of such constructs. It is style and genre and form and thematic disposition that the musical discourse invariably takes to be semantically substantive and necessary to any general critique of musical meaning.[39]

It is precisely these fundamental difficulties, however, that bring Schenker's analysis into play. The first point is more than suggestive: if nothing else,

38 In this regard, it is interesting that the most systematic attempts to reconstruct a theory of musical meaning in the early twentieth century are prompted by an interest in the Baroque Affektenlehre and Figurenlehre. See Arnold Schering, "Die Lehre von den musikalischen Figuren," *Kirchenmusikalisches Jahrbuch* 21 (1908), 106–114 and Hermann Kretzschmar, "Allgemeines und Besonderes zur Affektenlehre," *Jahrbuch der Musikbibliothek Peters für 1911* (1912), 1: 63–77; *1912* (1913), 2: 65–78. Schering's work on a musical hermeneutics can be traced from *Musikalische Bildung und Erziehung zum musikalischen Hören* (Leipzig: Quelle & Meyer, 1911; 4th edn. 1924) through *Das Symbol in der Musik* (Leipzig: Koehler und Amelung, 1941). Schenker has some familiarity with this work, as he dismisses Schering's textual additions to Beethoven Op. 106 in *Free Composition*, 133. We might even see the famous assignment of structural keys in Alfred Lorenz's *Das Geheimnis der Form bei Richard Wagner*, vol. 2, *Der musikalische Aufbau von Richard Wagners "Tristan und Isolde"* (Berlin: Max Hesse, 1926), 178, as deriving from eighteenth-century notions of the peculiar affect of keys.

39 This becomes very apparent when, as is most often the case, style is defined against a norm. The opposition of style and form mimics the division of semantics and syntax (or content and language). Inasmuch as the principal work in stylistics from the early twentieth century on has concentrated on the definition of personal styles, this conception is perhaps inevitable. A rather strange and philosophical investigation of style and meaning from Schenker's time is found in Siegfried Nadel, *Der duale Sinn der Musik* (Regensburg: Gustav Bosse, 1931).

Schenker holds a very specific historical slice of texts as his subject. The second point is more substantive. The historian cannot locate anything within the musical text itself which can stand as a grammatical function in the same way in which verb inflection and phonetics can for language. Yet this is exactly the role awarded performance by the nineteenth-century editor. Indeed, this role is necessarily entailed by the growing distance (both psychic and temporal) between composer and performer. When Riemann, to move expediently to the point, sets out a series of principles for executing texts musically, he is not thinking of these rules as giving meaning to the performance (that being within the province of the composer) but he is thinking of meaning as a means of guaranteeing that, in effect, the performer is speaking the same language as the composer. If, however, we are to assert that Riemann's rules guarantee such an accord between composer and performer, we must further admit that these rules likewise compel Beethoven, let us say, to speak (at least in form) the same language as Dunstable, Josquin, and Bach. In Riemann's practice, each of these composers' musics is subjected to the same principles of editing, thus performance, as construed by Riemann, is unavailable to the philological analysis.

This disability does not hold for Schenker. In moving the performance (or a carefully delineated representation of the dynamic shaping which makes for a performance) from outside of to inside the text, Schenker incorporates it into the language, as such, or into the text itself. He takes a convention of delivery and reworks it as a syntactic function. The embedded performance he locates in Mozart's text is not closer to the meaning of the passage than the artificial execution imposed by Riemann: to change Mozart's articulation is not to disturb or misread some semantic content, but rather to render the text ungrammatical. Likewise, the dynamic he locates in the subject of Bach's fugue stands outside of the meaning of the passage. We can, with little effort, think of Marx's kernel, his stepwise descent through a fourth in half-notes as potentially having all of the qualities of a musical text. We can even picture a context in which it is taken figuratively, assigned some conventional meaning. By contrast, Schenker's third-span is semantically empty. It unfolds in time, but not in rhythm. It is notated as a musical text, but could not be said to have a style. It determines a continuity but cannot be said to embody a musical form or schema. It is a music stripped of any qualities that could be said to have meaning, and hence a music that is purely grammatic.

Thus, we might (perhaps prematurely) conceive *Free Composition* as a comparative investigation of the interior performances intrinsic to a particular slice of musical texts, one in which Schenker arrives at a general taxonomy of inflections. We might quickly assume that this comparison entails that stratification that is the hallmark of Schenker's analysis and regard such as an empirically established history. However, lest we get too enthusiastic about this characterization, we need to admit that it fails rather spectacularly on a number of important points. We would not care to claim too strongly that Schenker locates distinct classes of musical texts, distinct languages as such. Nor would we make more than weak claims that he establishes, in any interesting way, a filiation of different texts or an original musical language or even any sort of chronology of musical languages (there being no particularly definable difference under Schenker's analysis between a piece by, let us say, Johann Bach and Johannes Brahms).

But even if we cannot assert that Schenker appropriates the comparative method in any manner that is dependably rigorous in lieu of being loosely heuristic, we still need not abandon the notion of philology. In fact, we might care to venture all of the claims of the preceding paragraph, though not use them in order to evidence a strict philological method. Instead, we might rather turn to an earlier point. We spoke previously of a matrix of assumptions held by the musical paleographer. We recall that under the fourth of these, the paleographer takes notation (or the physical appearance of the manuscript) as a potential window on a musical economy, in particular a window on the compositional process. For a medievalist, this might involve making a case for the successive rather than the simultaneous composition of lines, or vice versa. This point holds true for Schenker, with a twist. We might say that in bringing out the interior performance of the text Schenker opens a window on the improvisational imagination that figures so prominently in *Ornamentation*. To extrapolate from this statement, we might also say that for Schenker, if there is a historical dimension to the masterworks which can be opened philologically, it must define itself as a history of this imagination rather than a history of utterances fixed in notation – in other words, that within any plausible comparative analysis the notion of a musical language cannot be defined in terms of the specific text or group of texts or of any qualitative abstraction of such (style, genre, etc.) but must rather be defined in terms of the practice of improvisation.

While we might admire this extrapolation as a radical and sophisticated formulation, we might also, and with good reason, question whether it does not put the entire notion of a paleograpically sensitive Schenker at hazard, and ask whether, in seemingly shifting the historical presence of the analysis from the evidence of the text itself to the mechanics of the production of the text, this reading does not dissolve itself. Again, though, an earlier point leads us out of this difficulty. We need not assign Schenker the task of empirically establishing a history of music insomuch as he already holds to a narrative of that history, specifically to a narrative of the birth of the modern instrumental practice in the grand synthesis of earlier vocal practice and instrumental diminution with the coincident birth of modern harmony in the reconciliation of the horizontal and vertical dimensions in music. In fact, we may most profitably think of Schenker as appropriating the forms of philology (rather than its methodology) to substantiate this narrative.

Thus, we would first say that Schenker disentangles the internal dynamic of the masterwork − the interior performance, or better, composite of performances − in his later analysis in order to substantiate the historical presence of the text, reconstructing this presence as a series of grammatical statements or strata. The strategy of explaining a passage or even a whole work in terms of a series of operations is, of course, not new to the world of *Free Composition*. We might, in fact, trace it from the condensations of *Harmony* and the first volume of *Counterpoint* through such works as the analysis of the opening of Beethoven's Op. 101,[40] through such works as the analysis of Bach's fugue. We would, however, assert that these instances constitute only local unpackings and that it is only in the late analysis that this unpacking becomes systematic.

We would secondly assert that this systematicization is only plausible when conceived philologically, conceived in terms of a system of filiations in which an implicit genealogical tree of archetypical grammatic forms comes into being between a common original ancestor, the *Ursatz*, and the multiple texts of the canon.[41]

---

40 Heinrich Schenker, *Beethoven: Die letzten fünf Sonaten: kritische Ausgabe mit Einführung und Erläuterung: Sonata A dur Opus 101* (Vienna: Universal Edition, 1920; ed. Oswald Jonas, Vienna: Universal Edition, 1972), 52–53. Schenker's unpacking of the opening of this sonata resembles his unpacking of the C minor fugue theme.

41 In a philological method (in textual criticism, for example) two or more surviving witnesses are assumed to descend from a common hypothetical ancestor or archetype when they share a peculiar trait (usually in textual criticism an error or variant reading). By determining all such interrelationships or filiations between exemplars, and then between reconstructed archetypes, one can under the best of circumstances reconstruct a family tree (or stemma) leading to the original text. (These stemmas are often very complex.) We might thus think of the strata of any of Schenker's analyses as tracing a particular path back through an implied stemma which filiates all of the works of the canon. Interruption, for example, would thus constitute not a feature of a piece but an abstract reconstruction of the archetype for a whole class of pieces. Quite possibly there could be another

We would thirdly venture that this philological system substantiates (and is, in turn, validated by) a particular account of music history, one that stands for the most part at a distance from the standard historiography of music. By this reading Schenker may be said to see the central, living tradition of music to be improvisatory, and hence to see the notated artifacts of music history not as evidence of this tradition but as evidence of a second, peripheral, and artificial musical tradition.[42] Thus, the interior performances within the masterwork trace a history which is beyond historiography. The *Ursatz*, the originating musical statement or utterance, bears record of that moment when the vocal sound or noise is first shaped, first distinguished as an extraordinary human activity, as music.[43] The stratum of

subfamily of texts which do not descend from the interruption archetype, but which share with it the *Ursatz* as a common ancestor. Interpreted this way, *Free Composition* is not a catalogue or taxonomy of embellishments (as is the seventeenth-century diminutional treatise) but an attempt to establish the outlines of such a genealogy or stemma, and the *Ursatz* not an ideological assertion but a methodological convention of this system of filiations, a necessary common ancestor. See Maas, *Textual Criticism*, pp. 2–9 for a concise explanation of stemmatics.

42 This may be suggested in the following passage: "True song is given to diminution. It is born with the movement in seconds of the fundamental line, and develops further life through the seconds of the lines which evolve from it. So it sings its way through all these seconds, the conveyors of the melodic, into the foreground and within it further and further. All the manifold experience of the lines – which are none other than our experiences – are transformed into song. Wherefore then words to generate music, to point up its meaning, when music organically lives, sings, and speaks? Its inner song elevates absolute diminution above word-generated diminution, which is eternally chained to 'love,' 'hate,' and 'jealousy' " (*Free Composition*, 98). The notion of an improvisatory tradition standing outside of the written tradition of music, and even overshadowing this written tradition, would be familiar to Schenker through his study of seventeenth- and eighteenth-century diminutional practices. He could well have been aware, however, of older evidence of improvisatory practices. We recall that he speaks in the *Harmonielehre* of the artistic imagination rebelling against the false restraints of the system of church modes and liturgical restrictions (*Harmony*, 55–76). This notion (or similar notions) could easily be supported through the examination of theoretic sources from the Medieval period made available in C.-E.-H. Coussemaker's *Scriptorum de musica medii aevi novam seriem* (Paris: Durand, 1864–1876) which consistently yield a picture of theoretic attempts to regulate improvisatory practices. While we have little evidence that Schenker is substantively interested in music theories before Fux, he could well have been familiar with Riemann's history of theory, the introduction to which speaks of the birth of polyphony in an improvised practice. See Hugo Riemann, *Geschichte der Musiktheorie im IX.–XIX. Jahrhundert* (Leipzig: Max Hesse, 1898; 2nd edn. 1921). Note the nationalist rhetoric.

43 Schenker's notion of the *Ursatz* has been linked to the notion of an original form which is part of Goethe's biology. Yet it admits this other reading. The notion of an origin of music goes back to Condillac and Rousseau and their respective applications of Locke's epistemology of sensation and association to the problem of music, and continues (in various forms) to crop up through the nineteenth and early twentieth centuries. The first portion of the twentieth century speaks of the origins of music much differently than did the eighteenth century, however. Rather than standing as the inevitable beginning of a history, it now stands as the beginning of an activity or function. The question as to why music comes into being is posed anthropologically rather than

interruption records that time when two such sounds or noises are shaped into a single line and succeeding strata record the increasing inflection and modulation of such lines.[44] Where this improvised tradition surfaces, where it is finally evidenced in writing, not fortuitously coincides with (trivially) the abandonment of tablature notation and (importantly) with the formation of tonality. The agency whereby this unwritten tradition is made visible, however, the catalyst whereby it is precipitated in a notated form, is the seventeenth- and eighteenth-century practice of instrumental diminution. The whole of Schenker's stemma is thus anchored at one end by the abstract history of the *Ursatz* and at the other by the concrete history of diminution.

In theory, this synthesis should bring both histories under scrutiny. We might assert that the practice of diminution can only itself be truly examined (rather than simply and incompletely tabulated) when it is situated within the context of the deeper examination of the notion of performance. Again, this point can be supported through a counter-demonstration. One might derive a simple contrapuntal point of imitation from the pitches given on the strong beats of the fugue subject (Ex. 13). The case might be made that this reduction more plausibly illustrates Schenker's history of instrumental diminution on vocal models. What generalizations about diminution would arise from a reduction which posited a true (if

philosophically. For example, Karl Bücher's *Arbeit und Rhythmus* (Leipzig: Teubner, 1899) makes the case that music arises out of the need to coordinate work. This argument might seem far removed from that of Schenker, yet it is not unreasonable to think of the *Ursatz* as recovering the origin of music as an activity (if not its function). Two texts speak of the origins of music have been previously cited, Wallaschek's *Anfänge der Tonkunst* (which contains an interesting discussion of "time sense") and Stumpf's *Anfänge der Musik*. For a slightly different version see also Bernhard Hoffmann, *Kunst und Vogelgesang* (Leipzig: Quelle & Meyer, 1908). Schenker does speak of the tonally incoherent origins of music in the *Harmonielehre* (*Harmony*, 53) and at various places in his later work.

44 Schenker clearly distinguishes the character of different broad strata in *Der freie Satz*. The *Ursatz* can only occur in one stratum (although similar configurations can occur in subordinate strata), interruption in another. This distinction may, however, be more methodological than substantive – hence the difficulty in defining the abstraction of Schenker's levels. The background is given by stipulation, yet it is only a less complex form of behavior than the middleground and foreground, with their repetitions, prolongations, transformations, unwindings, dissolutions, recastings, and reshapings. It might also be objected that Schenker gives a whole variety of fundamental constructs, initiating the *Ursatz* variously at the third, fifth, and octave, and awarding it various supports in the lower register. I would argue that the pregnancy of the original moment of performance allows for this variety, that Schenker is able to conceive such a variety of constructions because the essence of the *Ursatz* lies in its dynamic rather than its pitch. For a very interesting reading of Schenker's notion of strata, see Gregory Proctor and Herbert Riggens, "Levels and the Reordering of Chapters in Schenker's *Free Composition*," *Music Theory Spectrum* 10 (1988), 102–126.

hypothetical) musical text lying behind the given surface? We might attempt similar reductions on other fugal expositions, gather our results and posit some mechanics of embellishment, and maybe on this basis establish some sort of diminutional taxonomy. We might attempt to relate our diminutional taxonomy with those of the period. We might go so far as to extend our comparison to different portions of the fugue or to passages of like or unlike tempo, or even to passages extracted from different instrumental genres, and thus give some flexibility to the notion of embellishment. The problem with this program is, however, that the logic behind our procedure is circular: the reduction itself already presumes at least an unexamined and intuitive grasp of what constitutes the model and what the diminution. It is this circularity which is avoided in Schenker's analysis: the mechanics of diminution can be put under scrutiny with a degree of confidence because model and embellishment differ in kind, the former standing before notation, the latter standing within notation.

In practice, the join between these two histories has been so smoothed over as to be almost imperceptible. The analysis is constituted as a continuum in which the mapping of interior performances (in terms of normative pitch structures) blends almost without notice into the concrete luxuriance of embellishment. Even at the remote origin represented by the *Ursatz* it reflects the contrapuntal nature of the surface of the text (the pitches in the analysis, although changing function, still align with those of the text) and hence the sequence from background to foreground seemingly reflects a process of elaboration or diminution (although again, Schenker does insist on the autonomy of various strata) and hence even the stratum of the analysis which lies closest to the surface of the text is at least to a certain degree abstract or performative.

This leads us to venture a closing point. One puts forward the notion of a paleographic and philologic Schenker with a certain trepidation. Obviously this latter reading is at odds with Schenker's occasional assertion (at least in regard to compositional process) that he does not intend the movement from *Ursatz* to textual surface to be read chronologically.[45] We

---

45 "The forms of the fundamental structure, derived from the masterworks, might give cause for misunderstanding to young artists, who are mainly dependent upon imitation. Specifically, the following question could arise: need one only vary some fundamental structure in order to arrive at the foreground of, say, a symphony? Whoever asks this introduces the notion of time sequence, a "chronology of creation" into the idea of the fundamental structure <and the transformation levels>. This notion is not correct. The concept of the fundamental structure by no means claims to provide specific information about the chronology of creation; it presents only the *strictly logical*

Example 13

Example 13 (cont.)

might argue that our reading of a philological Schenker makes exactly this point, that it is as impossible to reproduce the compositional workings of the masters as it would be to reproduce the historical reserve that lies behind their works. More generally, though, we would reemphasize the rather formidable historical sensibility found throughout Schenker's writings. Far beyond the other theorists of his generation, he takes seriously the abandoned compositional procedures of species counterpoint and figured bass, and is the sole theorist to assert a historically correct notion of diminution. (We would all remember that point of enlightenment held in common by all students of Schenker's works where "diminution" ceases to be taken as a reduced-value statement of a fugue subject.)

The most telling evidence of a historicist Schenker is almost too obvious, though. Without doubt, most of Schenker's theoretical contemporaries would have held to some version of a canon of late eighteenth- and nineteenth-century instrumental works. In this regard, Schenker himself would attract notice only through his dogged fidelity to this canon, an attitude that we would rightly (if too conveniently) read as a symptom of a rather extreme ideology. In fact, we might use this point to argue against a historicist Schenker since, after all, the new empirical sciences of musicology most spectacularly open windows on musics standing outside of this canon both historically and culturally. We might also argue the opposite: Schenker's canon, as noted before, suggests a philology inasmuch as it is a slice (albeit a thick one) of the historical substance of music and can thus be examined under the comparative method. We would expand this point. In distinguishing his canon from emerging musics (be they the Medieval or Renaissance musics recovered by the musicologists or, in particular, the musics of composers after Brahms), Schenker cannot content himself with the simple description of those qualities that set this canon apart; he cannot simply gauge it against some autonomous body of theoretic standards, but must account for its particular character by defining it theoretically as a unique historical phenomenon, a unique historical

precision in the relationship between simple tone-successions and more complex ones" (*Free Composition*, 18 – angle brackets enclose an editorial insertion by Oster). But also, more philosophically: "In the secret perception of the interactions of origin, development, and present, as well as in the cultivation of this awareness until it becomes definite knowledge, lies what we call tradition: the conscious handing down, passing on of all relatedness which flows together into the wholeness of life. To the person who is vitally aware of such relatedness, an idea is also part of real life, be that idea religion, art, science, law, the state. Therefore the principle of origin, development, and present as background, middleground, and foreground applies also to the life of the idea within us" (*Free Composition*, 3).

moment. Thus, his history has less in common with that of the archivist and more in common with that of the political economist.[46]

In other words, in assuming that what is most important or essential in the history of music is beyond recovery by the empirical methods of the musicologist, and also in refusing to conceive of his theory as an autonomous or neutral analytic system against which to evaluate an undefined span of recovered or future musics, Schenker abandons or (at least) sets aside the conception of historiography as a descriptive discipline. In coopting the form of philology and (if covertly) embedding it in the structure of his analysis, he appropriates the authority of that most central of nineteenth-century historical sciences to the service of a history that does not report but which rather explains. We might venture so far as to say that he turns the relation between work and context on its head, that he does not use the history of music (or an empirically founded historical context) to define his canon but rather uses that canon as the point from which to construct his own history. Furthermore, we would see this substitution of a critical or embedded history for a scientific or contextual historiography, of explanation for description, as a strategy (and one strongly enhanced by its appropriation of paleography and philology) through which Schenker's theory can claim to hold its own against the empirical authority of the new musicology.

46 Foucault speaks at length of the economics of David Ricardo as introducing the notion of history into the examination of labor and exchange. In the case of Ricardo, this history is one accumulating value in combination with continuing scarcities culminating finally in a static balance of production and consumption (*The Order of Things*, 253–263). Schenker's history of music is in many ways similar. He in effect derives the history of music from a discrepancy between an innate artistic impulse and ways (be they theoretical or notational or instrumental) of realizing this impulse. Musical practice is always in rebellion against musical theory, which in turn attempts to recapture that practice, which again attempts to escape the bonds of theory. In other words, the history of music is cumulative, until it reaches the point at which musical practice reaches the limit of the artistic impulse. Thus the history of music ends with the canon (but, considering that theory lags behind practice, it in turn reaches its limit and the history of theory reaches its end in Schenker's own work). This conception of a finite history likewise has a resonance in the idea of origins (and hence has some bearing on the notion of the *Ursatz*). Foucault discusses the situation of the nineteenth-century conception of origins at length, arguing that it is necessary to the view of a culminating history – and Schenker's history, with its denial of the possibility of composition after the master, is just such a history (*The Order of Things*, 328–335).

3

THE OBJECTIVE SYNTHESIS

THE COORDINATION OF DISCOURSES

We now have two readings of Schenker, each of which addresses a strategy for appropriating and then subsuming the authority of the new musical sciences of the later nineteenth century – a strategy involving the seeming reversal of discursive modes substituting, on the one hand, a descriptive and analytic psychology of music for the experiments and hypotheses of the psychoacoustician and, on the other, an explanatory and constructivist history of music for the historiography of the musicologist. The natural progression of our argument is obvious: while each of these readings may in turn be less than satisfying as an explication of why Schenker makes such strong claims in his later analysis and of how he satisfies these claims, we would assert that such an explication is within reach through a combination of these two readings.

But we let ourselves off of the hook too easily. Neither reading seems adequately to engage the question of definite purpose and intention. In other words, neither reading tells us why Schenker has done what we think he has done. We cannot bolster each of these readings individually in this regard: each argument must stand as it is. Thus, in examining the reconciliation of Schenker's two strategies, we need to search for a broader epistemology, one which itself can explicate his intention and purpose.

To this end, we would first conceive of these readings a bit differently. We would hope to prove that Schenker's mature analysis is truly a complex argument. Each of our readings describes a trajectory through Schenker's work, from *Harmony* and *Ornamentation* to this complex argument, to *Free Composition*. We might, however, think of this motion as a single trajectory determined by two functions, and in order to trace this motion we might look to ways in which the respective discourses of theory and history participate in a series of transactions throughout Schenker's work, thus arriving at evidence of purpose or intent in a manner more simple.

As noted, there are several points of engagement between Schenker's historical and psycho-theoretical inquiries. In *Ornamentation* he makes a point of updating C. P. E. Bach's taxonomy of ornamentation by examining the "psychological content" of each figural class, and he puts forward a case for the historical appropriateness of species counterpoint in the first volume of *Counterpoint*. Species counterpoint in itself constitutes a circumscribed taxonomy of diminution. In representing the interior performance by a normative pitch structure (usually a descent, albeit in combination with some indication of grouping), we automatically suppose that a historical construction can be taken as an efficient description of a perceptual phenomenon, and thus suppose that Schenker is simply assigning a priority to the psychological content specified by the specific construction.

We might more profitably attempt to fix these points of engagement within a system of coordinations and compensations that seems to operate throughout those of Schenker's works to which we have made reference. First, both *Ornamentation* and *Harmony* fit easily within the accustomed modes of writing about music despite their respective claims radically to correct the musical discourse. *Ornamentation*, after all, is constituted as the critical apparatus appended to Schenker's edition of C. P. E. Bach keyboard works, and *Harmony* is but one of an embarrassment of harmony texts dating from the last decades of the nineteenth century and the first decade of the twentieth. What is truly radical in these works is not the form or genre, but the attempts to locate the empirical or scientific edges of their respective discourses. *Ornamentation* thus appropriates the suppositions and methodologies of historical musicology in order to explicate a musical sensibility that, while alien, lies much closer in time to the classical canon than to those historic sensibilities normally examined by the medievalist; and *Harmony*, not content simply to invoke psychoacoustics as a justification for triadic harmony, hypothesizes (in its discussion of harmonic prolongation) the existence of a new and explanatorily powerful perceptual mechanism.

Schenker, as briefly noted, cross-addresses these works. At its close, *Ornamentation* attempts a psycho-theoretic treatment of ornament by bringing to the surface a collection of perceptual mechanisms underlying different classes of embellishment, and *Harmony* awards the modern tonal system a development or history (albeit one of artistic impulse rebelling against false authority). In neither case, however, is this reference necessary. *Ornamentation* does not need to argue the theoretic substantiation of embellishment and *Harmony* does not need to argue the defects of the modal system. Each work speaks to a distinct discursive community, and while the author might find it desirable to recognize a complementation or coordination between these two works, he would not think to challenge the notion of two distinct and autonomous discourses, the first historical and the second theoretical (and by extension psychological).

With the first volume of *Counterpoint*, however, this distribution of tasks has perhaps become slightly problematic for Schenker. We might see an attempt to remedy an asymmetry holding between its two predecessors in this work, in particular between their respective epistemologies. *Ornamentation* holds closely to the empirical surety of musicological method. As a work of music theory, *Harmony* cannot claim such empirical surety. We would be tempted, therefore, to see *Counterpoint* I as an attempt to restore a balance, to correct *Harmony*. By treating species counterpoint as a laboratory, Schenker can affiliate this work more closely with the promised certainties of physiological acoustics and the psychology of perception and thus would put his theoretic project on a more equal footing with his historical project.

Yet the first volume of *Counterpoint* does more than simply correct a balance. While Schenker claims to have given counterpoint a priority over harmony all along, and to have published a harmony treatise first solely for reasons of expediency, we may be forgiven for doubting his account.[1] Setting aside our own prejudices, the turn from harmony to counterpoint (in particular to species counterpoint) would have seemed at the time a return to an obsolete or pedantic theory. Also, though, it is a turn (as we have already noted) to a discipline that has tangible historical ramifications. In other words, the evidence that Schenker draws from earlier theorists about the perception of pitch constructions is (at least implicitly) evidence of a peculiar historic sensibility. While the first volume of *Counterpoint* overtly claims to set theory on the new ground of a more powerful explanatory psychology, it covertly moves to coordinate and, in fact, even to an extent consolidate the respective discourses of theory and music history.

Perhaps we oversimplify when we speak of consolidation. Schenker's reading of Bach's fugue shows the peculiarity of his relation to these

---

1   Interestingly, this claim is made in the introduction to the second volume of *Counterpoint* (p. xii). It would seem that by this time he has come to see the scale-step as something to be established after voice-leading.

respective discourses. Remarkable as is this work, we might overlook the fact that Schenker frames his argument against a historical notion of fugue as a genre. Indeed, his case rests upon the thesis that Bach's fugue transcends its genre not by virtue of its brilliant application of those techniques (double and invertible counterpoint, the general schema of fugue or the rhetoric of imitation) that distinguish the composition of the fugue as a historical practice, but rather because of an internal dynamic which is almost obscured by Bach's technical mastery.

We might likewise be tempted to argue that Schenker's attempt in reading the fugue to reconstruct a musical sensibility that lies anterior to such devices as statements, imitations, episodes, and inversion also constitutes an argument against music theory. While we might not be able to make a convincing case for this notion, it does suggest a similarly complex reading of the second volume of *Counterpoint*. We have previously confessed some unease with the position of *Counterpoint* II, yet in arguing Schenker's explication of Bach's fugue as a theoretization of his historical project we would be tempted to argue *Counterpoint* II as a compensatory historicization of his theoretical practice. In other words, we might read this work as extending not the epistemological agenda of *Counterpoint* I but rather its historical correctness. In fact, we might even read it as an attempt to recapture that exact temporal moment wherein instrumental diminution gives rise to a new music, explaining thus to ourselves the discussion of "bridges to free composition" which concludes *Counterpoint* II, yet whose possibility is so vehemently denied in *Counterpoint* I.

Given time, we could undoubtedly examine other works by Schenker and in doing so refine our understanding of the various compensations and synchronizations of historical and theoretical projects that form his discursive trajectory. Yet even with the limited evidence of our survey to this point, we note that Schenker increasingly addresses the respective discourses of music history and theory rather obliquely. It would appear to become difficult for him to avoid a subtle and developing conflation of his different agendas. We might imagine any number of such conflations of the historical and the theoretical, yet what we find in Schenker seems to have a peculiar quality – as already stated, a peculiar obliqueness. Our general thesis – the notion that Schenker's development is epistemologically driven – provides a satisfying explanation for this quality. We would venture that Schenker increasingly addresses distinct communities, not in regard to their particular discourse but by the empiricism which they hold in common.

This explication again, however, does not bear directly on intention or purpose. Perhaps we may come to discover a (temporarily) preferable explication by situating Schenker's discursive conflation within a general context.

SYSTEM AND SYNTHESIS

It will come as no surprise that we revisit the indefatigable Hugo Riemann in our attempt to elucidate this context. As noted, Riemann allies his work quite conspicuously with the new musical sciences of the later nineteenth century. This move is but part of a general project to systematize the musical discourse: in bringing the various genres of music writing under the aegis of the new empiricism, Riemann wishes to interconnect the various localities of the musical sciences and in doing so to endow the whole with consistency and universality.[2] The extent of this systematicization is truly ambitious. Psychoacoustics, or the study of musical perception, is incorporated into the construction of music theory through notions of harmonic dualism and harmonic functionalism; theory is itself further bound to performance practice through the systematic treatment of rhythm and phrasing as well as through various editorial activities; theory is likewise bound to musical historiography through an extensive examination of the history of theory and through the narrative of a developing harmonic sensibility; and musicology is likewise awarded an extra-historical rigor

---

2 The universality of the eighteenth-century musical discourse is given tangible form in the encyclopedia. Riemann's most concise statement of the system of musical study is found in the *Grundriss der Musikwissenschaft*. Two articles from around this time which discuss Riemann's attempt to construct a coherent and universal musical discourse are (in relation to historic musicology) Wilibald Gurlitt, "Hugo Riemann und die Musikgeschichte...Erster Teil: Voraussetzungen," *Zeitschrift für Musikwissenschaft* 1 (1919): 571–587, and Herbert Eimert, "Bekenntnis und Methode: Zur gegenwärtigen Lage der Musikwissenschaft" in *Zeitschrift für Musikwissenschaft* 9 (1926): 95–109. Potter speaks of the exemplary position of Riemann in the various attempts to rethink the discipline of musicology (Trends in German Musicology, 6). The most sustained and sophisticated modern attempt to rationalize a universal discursive system for music (or repair this discursive rupture) is found in Jean-Jacques Nattiez's *Fondements d'une sémiologie de la musique* (Paris: Union générale d'éditions, 1975). Nattiez comes at this problem theoretically, parsing the musical act between a poetic level (the domain of the composer), a neutral level (the domain of the work) and an "esthesic" level (the domain of the audience). Thus any particular investigation of music can be situated within this economy (see the diagram, *Fondements*, 60). Nattiez returns to the same ground more reflectively in *Music and Discourse: Toward a Semiology of Music*, trans. Carolyn Abbate (Princeton: Princeton University Press, 1990). This outstanding piece of work touches on many of the same issues and works (such as Lomax) discussed in this text (although from a different perspective).

through the application of the modern performance apparatus to the transcription of musical texts.

For the record, though, this grand agenda comes to naught. The attempt to ground functional harmony in some empirically based theory fails or is abandoned soon after the turn of the century; the systematic treatment of rhythm and performance is attacked by the next generation as mechanical; and his renovation of old music is likewise seen by his successors as irretrievably tainted. One after another, each of Riemann's attempts to systematize musical studies is seen to fail (a failure we ourselves would attribute to the inherent autonomy or independence of the truly empirical studies of music), and it need come as no surprise that by the close of his life Riemann has sequestered himself in the pure and epistemologically transparent domain of Byzantine studies.[3]

Riemann is not the sole figure to entertain such a notion of a universal system of musical investigations – one immediately recalls the attempts of such figures as Guido Adler to order the proliferation of the new sciences – yet he is the figure who most avidly attempts, in his own work, to substantiate his system, and we can take his failure to be symptomatic of a more general event in the musical discourse of the early twentieth century. Indeed, we would be given to understand that it is this failure in large part that prompts the pregnant notion of a divide between *Naturwissenschaft* and *Geisteswissenschaft* which figures so importantly in the post-war politics of the academy.[4] We might instinctively isolate Schenker from this failure,

3 I have earlier made reference to the rejection of Riemann's harmony and to the turn from his method of interpretive transcription to one more authentic. The "Ideen zu einer 'Lehre von den Tonvorstellungen'" is substantially an apology for his psychologistic theory. In many other areas Riemann seems on the defensive after the turn of the century. He defends his psychological theory of rhythm and his ideas about the performance of chant against Dom Mocquereau's ideas on the subject in "Ein Kapital vom Rhythmus" in *Die Musik* 3/15 (May 1904), 155–162. Likewise he defends his readings of Medieval secular monophony against newer readings in "Die Beck–Aubry'sche 'modale Interpretation' der Troubadourmelodien" in *Sammelbände der Internationalen Musik-Gesellschaft* (1909–1910), 569–589. While it is not strictly true that Riemann closets himself in the comfortable domain of Byzantine studies at the end of his career (two of his last works are a study of folkloristic tonality and a collection of analyses of Beethoven sonatas), the most intensive and original works of Riemann's old age are *Die byzantinische Notenschrift im 10. bis 15. Jahrhundert* (Leipzig: Breitkopf und Härtel, 1909) and *Neue Beiträge zur Lösung der Probleme der byzantinischen Notenschrift* (Leipzig: Breitkopf und Härtel, 1915).

4 Potter (Trends in German Musicology) reads this crisis, again, as one pitting the advocates of the study of music as a *Geisteswissenschaft* against the advocates of a *Naturwissenschaft*. The positivists held the upper hand before the First World War, the advocates of a Diltheyan method the upper hand after the war. In the 1930s, the positivists regained ground, although at the cost of being (to some extent) coopted by National Socialism. Potter cites a number of interesting programs for

arguing either his provinciality in relation to the work of the great figures of academia or his sophistication in avoiding a rather naive and unthinking enthusiasm held by those less gifted than himself. From the first, after all, the affiliations he draws between his own work and the empirical studies of comparative musicology and the psychology of perception are more guarded than those of Riemann. He never overtly attempts to justify or weight his work by invoking some authority outside the limited circle of music theorists. If, however, we are to accept that the affiliations of Schenker's early works are, if anything, more radical than those of Riemann (or of any other of his contemporaries), and that the respective prefaces and introductions of Schenker's works evidence a striking theoretical appreciation of the demands and consequences of the new musical empiricisms of the later nineteenth century, we might rather situate his development within instead of without the effort to draw together the disparate strands of musical discourse, and we might thus ascribe a particular motivation to the various subsumptions, compensations, and coordinations we have sketched in his work.

Yet if we are to attribute to Schenker the intention of reintegrating a fragmented economy of musical discourse, we cannot expect to find this program put into execution through some systematization. His path, like his appeal to the empirical science, cannot but be more sophisticated.

Here, however, we may be inclined towards an obvious if oblique reading of this reintegration. We would perhaps note that Schenker from the earliest voices his most urgent thoughts about music in a series of meditations that vaguely connect with the language of idealist philosophy.[5] By contrast, we

---

musicology which arose from this debate. Speaking pragmatically, however, one feels that the ordinary practicing musicologist would have acknowledged (to some degree) both sides of the argument, and that the vehemence of this debate is a result of a more general (if inevitable) failure to establish a sytematic program for musical investigation.

5   Schenker indulges rather easily in the philosophical rhetoric of his time, yet in actuality he seems to have for the most part only a second- or third-hand acquaintance with the specifics of philosophy and aesthetics. He is comfortable quoting safely remote figures such as Goethe or Burkhart, but does not affiliate his project directly with any of the critical philosophers, going so far as to disparage Schopenhauer on occasion (*Counterpoint* I, 15–16; *Free Composition*, f.n. xxiv). Perhaps he could have been influenced by the Hegelian notion of a "philosophy in practice," and his political and social views are definitely in accord with a Right-Hegelianism, yet one would not wish to take this line of thought too far. The neo-Kantian movement of the latter part of the nineteenth century and early portion of the twentieth century is bound up with the rebirth of epistemology as a philosophic project, and involves a very complex interchange between different schools. Schenker's writings do not show any trace of this epistemology. He might, however, have been familiar with

cannot immediately recall an instance in which he approvingly cites any historical musicologist or psycho-musical theorist. Thus, while not denying Schenker's early engagements with the empirical disciplines of music, we might see them as tentative, even begrudging overtures to what were, in fact, the most authoritative musical discourses of the time – overtures which, after the trauma of the defeat of Austro-Hungary and Germany in the war, came to seem irrelevant or encumbering and which seemed no longer to promise a strong and exclusive validation of the superiority of Germanic culture. We might read Schenker's later work not as a deepening or a development of earlier epistemological concerns but rather as an abandonment of the trappings of the musical sciences in favor of a purer and more powerful discourse grounded in idealistic philosophy, a discourse which, standing above the various sciences of music, promises to heal all rifts. Or, more cynically, we might read into this motion a simple rebellion against the authority figures of Schenker's musical youth, a reading reinforced by his consistent disdain for what he takes to be the musical establishment.

Of course, to sustain this reading would be to undermine much of our argument. Thus, we would point out that the notion of an idealist Schenker is awkward on three counts. First, and most generously, it underestimates Schenker's engagement with the sciences of music in his early work. It may seem at first sufficient to dismiss his references to the "psychology of tones" or to the original text as fashionable gestures yet, as we have noted, these engagements profoundly structure such work as *Ornamentation* and the first volume of *Counterpoint* and it would seem implausible that he would abandon such investments altogether. Second, a Schenker who simply rebelled against the positivist authorities of his youth would more likely than not have completely abandoned the technical aspect of his project, and would have come, in all likelihood, to see historiography and theory as merely the preparations for some philosophical quest for the musical essence (as did the Romantic critics). In other words, he would have ceased doing work that bore resemblance to some traditional notion of music theory. Third, to accept a reading of the later Schenker that turns upon a supposed rejection of the epistemological reasoning of the earlier Schenker

one of the several texts which recapitulated the philosophic discourse of music. See Paul Moos, *Die Philosophie der Musik* (Stuttgart: Deutsche Verlags-Anstalt, 2nd edn. 1922) and Felix Gatz's anthology *Musik-Ästhetik in ihren Hauptrichtungen* (Stuttgart: Ferdinand Enke, 1929).

would be to set those claims that he makes on the disciplines of performance, the writing of the history of music, and the development of the musical ear beyond effective scrutiny.

There is something in the picture of an idealist Schenker, however, that merits attention. The forms within which Schenker's works address various musical communities become progressively more complex. This increasing complexity is motivated by a desire (shared with Riemann and others) to reintegrate independent strands of the musical discourse. Schenker's attempt takes shape against a failure (on the part of Riemann and others) to configure this reintegration systemically. The culmination of this project is to be seen in Schenker's later analysis – the solution to the problem of a fragmented discourse. The nature of this solution is to not be found in any introductory or programmatic briefs in, let us say, *Free Composition*, but in Schenker's rhetoric of the ideal. Schenker, by the close of his career, makes strong ontological claims for the "masterwork." He speaks of it in the most elevated of terms as an artistic synthesis, ideally in its simultaneous embodiment of maximum freedom and maximum discipline, substantively in its reconciliation of the vertical and horizontal musical dimensions, historically (as we have noted) in its conflation of instrumental diminution and vocal counterpoint. Alien as is this term to our analysis, and strangely loaded as it is, we cannot avoid speaking of Schenker's later work itself as a synthesis, not an artistic but an epistemological synthesis, a motion within which a descriptive psychology and an explanatory history are mapped upon each other, reconciled, subsumed, transcended, as are composition and performance practices (inasmuch as composition embodies interior performances) and notated and improvisatory practices (inasmuch as the interior of the text reconstructs a musical tradition uncaptured by notation).

CLOSURE

While we may accept the desire for some sort of epistemological synthesis as the motivation for the various compensations and coordinations noted in Schenker's work, the notion of "synthesis" itself, as part of its idealist legacy, resists examination. Thus, we might, for now, let it remain unexamined, and simply remark that it is this turn from a systemic to a synthetic reintegration of the available musical discourses rather than an idealist rhetoric which most logically leads to the intellectual abandon of his later works. In fact, this rhetoric can be constructed from an extrapolation of the notion of synthesis to govern or dissolve a potentially infinite (and vertiginous) series of oppositions implicit in the musical discourse. Three open upon striking areas of Schenker's rhetoric. The later analysis, if only implicitly, locates a point at which the two broadest constructions of human culture are reconciled, the biological and the anthropological (of which psychology and history are but local manifestations). Likewise, it fixes a subsumption of production and consumption, of composition and reception. Likewise, as well, it collapses the distinction between synchrony and diachrony: it is a reading of (and only of) a specific slice of the history of music, or of a group of texts that occupy a specific moment, while at the same time it does not demand of the listener that she or he reenact this moment, or demand any distancing authenticity.

The first of these syntheses seems almost too broad, until the evidence of Schenker's political and social pronouncements is taken into account.[6] Again, the specifics of Schenker's ideology lie outside the brief of this essay. However, its place or function within his discourse cannot be ignored. Most commonly, if least honestly, this ideology or social program is taken as something distinguishable from the substance of the theory. In other words, it is a disability from which the theory must be shielded. With more sophistication, and more honesty, this potential for embarrassment can be engaged directly and the theory can be treated as a collection of symptoms or a superstructure of Schenker's politics. On the other hand, a contrary reading is suggested by the notion of an extrapolated synthesis of the biological and anthropological constructions of experience. While not denying Schenker his social convictions, we can take the increasing urgency of the political digressions in his writings as a symptom of this synthesis. More directly, it is only when Schenker feels himself to be in command of a sophisticated (indeed transcendent) epistemology and a uniquely powerful analysis of music that he can dissolve any remaining barriers between his polemic and the musical text.

The second of these syntheses might seem trivial inasmuch as any theory

6   It is only by reference to the particular context in which Schenker is writing that we can postulate
    such a broad synthesis. He all too frequently makes recourse to biological metaphors, and implicitly
    extends these metaphors to explicate not simply musical behaviour but culture at large. On a rather
    dark note, we should remember that this was the period when notions of race (itself a synthesis of
    the biological and the anthropological) come to the fore. Potter is particularly good on this angle
    (Trends in German Musicology, 59–89). It would be very interesting to see whether a close reading
    of Schenker would support (as I would expect) an implicit rejection of the equation of race and
    culture.

of music must claim to locate a mediating structure between composer and audience.[7] What is striking in Schenker's writings, though, is that this mediation does not (unlike that of his eighteenth-century predecessors) ultimately rest on the general stipulation of a natural and universal order of music (in the case of the eighteenth century on the representation of whole-number acoustics in harmony and the general imitation of the passions). Indeed, one can read the attempts of such later nineteenth-century theorists as Riemann to reground theory in empiricism as a failed attempt to recover such an order. Schenker, by contrast, restricts himself to a limited body of works from which to demystify the compositional process. While he sacrifices the individual intention of the composer in order to construct a general analysis in common with all theory, he is able to represent composition as an activity rather than as an abstract collection of rules and precepts, and link this representation to a theory of reception. However, to make the activity of composition his subject, he is led to deny effectively any compositional activity that stands outside of the canon of masterworks.

The third synthesis, that of the synchronic and diachronic, or of a historical and an ahistorical experience of music, is in some ways the most opaque. Unpacking it requires the reenlistment of a figure who has remained mute for some time. In the opening of this essay, Schenker's turn from the overt psychologism of *Harmony* and the first volume of *Counterpoint* was linked to Dilthey's call for the replacement of an explanatory and constructivist psychology by a psychology that is descriptive and analytic as the ground for the study of the human sciences. Inasmuch as Dilthey is by vocation a historian, it might have seemed logical not only to enlist Dilthey in the discussion of Schenker's historicism but to argue Schenker's synthesis of psychology and history as a fulfillment, within the domain of music, of Dilthey's program.

There is one particular problem with this argument, however, a problem that turns on Schenker's idealist rhetoric. Despite a certain kinship, Dilthey and Schenker define the objects of their respective investigations very differently. Dilthey fixes his agenda on the creation of a psychology (and

---

7 That is to say, many theories are prescriptive: they locate for the composer (or the student of music in general) a sort of consensus on the possibilities of music. The theorization of the relation between composer and performer or audience lies, as noted, at the heart of Nattiez's semiotics wherein the musical work itself, existing in a neutral ground, mediates the poetic (compositional) and esthesic (receptive) creations of musical meaning. The problematization of the relation between composer and audience centers also Adorno's sociology (although quite differently).

hence a history) that maps the "nexus of lived experience." In the preface to *Harmony*, Schenker claims to explicate the "interior life of the tones."[8] On first reading, one notes a coincidence of terminology, and may read the latter as an anthropological trope of the former (a trope, though, directly indebted to Schopenhauer). But on reflection, these formulas translate into contradictory agendas. Dilthey quite logically assigns priority within his program. The historiography he intends would (in principle, if not in practice) be contingent upon the construction of his descriptive and analytic psychology. Schenker, however, taking refuge in the idealistic formula of "the interior life of the tones", sets off his object of study, at least on the surface, from the human mentality and renders any notion of a fixed agenda suspect. Through this move he avoids assigning priority to either the diachronic or the synchronic analysis.

The stipulation of an "interior life of the tones" of itself would, yet, seem to threaten an epistemological reading in its entirety. If only to minimize this threat, we would assert that it plausibly accounts for the secrecy with which Schenker constructs a descriptive psychology and a philological structure. Yet Schenker's formula should not stand without challenge. All idealist rhetoric aside, Schenker is forced to delimit strictly the span of this "interior life of the tones" in order to give himself an explanatory purchase. Specifically, he cannot define this life as a property of music in general, but only as the property of a concrete body of texts: the canon of eighteenth- and nineteenth-century German (or Germanic) instrumental masterworks.

Here we find ourselves on very interesting ground. Earlier, we referred to the canon obliquely in speaking of the necessity of taking a historical slice out of music in order to construct a comparative examination. We, if

---

8 *Harmony*, xxv. We should not, of course, confuse Dilthey's "Erlebnis" ("experience") with Schenker's "Eigenleben." (I translate "Eigenleben" as "interior life" rather than "vitality" to bring it into accord with the philosophic discourse: Schenker eventually speaks of the same notion as "Tonwille.") One is not sure whether in *Harmony* he actually ascribes a life to the tones themselves, or whether (as in Schopenhauer) they represent life. In *Free Composition* he at one point seems to take the latter view, speaking of tones as images: "As the image of our life-motion, music can approach a state of objectivity, never, of course, to the extent that it need abandon its own specific nature as an art. Thus, it may almost evoke pictures or seem to be endowed with speech; it may pursue its course by means of associations, references, and connectives; it may use repetitions of the same tonal succession to express different meanings; it may simulate expectation, preparation, surprise, disappointment, patience, impatience, and humor" (p. 5). A few pages later, however: "Music is not only an *object* of theoretical consideration. It is *subject*, just as we ourselves are subject. Even the octave, fifth, and third of the harmonic series are a product of the organic activity of the tone as subject, just as the urges of the human being are organic. Accordingly, the quest for a new form of music is a quest for a homunculus" (p. 9).

but casually, also granted the canon an important function as a catalyst in his synthetic economy of composition and reception. Yet Schenker's adherence to the received canon (unlike, let us say, the notions of prolongation or structural levels) seems almost too obvious, too static, too much an ideological move to stand at the center of any modern reading of Schenker. Indeed, like Schenker's formulation of the "interior life of the tones," it too calls into question the assumption of an epistemological Schenker. Perhaps at their respective inceptions the musical sciences of the later nineteenth century were conceived as (potentially) authoritative validations of the accepted canon. By their very constitutions, however, by their universality (we remember Dilthey's "nexus of lived experience"), they cannot but undermine the ideology of the canon. In looking on the various historic musics as alien and autonomous (and in all probability being drawn to those musical traditions which seem most opaque), the historical musicologist will eventually come to see a rough equality of all musical traditions.[9] The empirical psychologist, on the other hand, while tempted by the idea that certain individuals (in particular the canonic composers) possess or possessed superior musical faculties, cannot but find those mechanisms of perception and reception common to the species as a whole a more available and urgent object of study.[10] One might locate the

9 Foucault makes this point in relation to philology (*The Order of Things*, 285). We might look at it from a different angle. Although there is a strong strain of music history writing in the nineteenth century which would see the entire history of music as a preparation for the present, the development of any more sophisticated historiological narratology cannot but lead to a rather different picture. Any narrative strategy or periodicization, be it one of exemplary figures or techniques, or one of ideal types or structural cycles, will come eventually to argue against a naive evolutionism and will force the historian (in order to form a complete sequence) to bring into play musics which are alien against musics which are familiar – hence such recuperative notions as the "Age of Scarlatti" or "High Gothic" or "Mannerism." In fact, the only way to truly avoid this is to sequester music history as some idealist abstraction (as does Schenker). Interestingly enough, there are attempts in the early twentieth century to arrive at structurally informed narratology, the most extreme example of which is Alfred Lorenz's *Abendländische Musikgeschichte im Rhythmus der Generationen* (Berlin: Max Hesse, 1928). For the standard account of musical historiography see Warren Dwight Allen, *Philosophies of Music History* (New York: American Book Co., 1939; 2nd edn. 1962).
10 There is a literature on the study of musical talent. We would note (from Schenker's time) Géza Révész, *The Psychology of a Musical Prodigy* [1916], trans. unattributed (New York: Harcourt, Brace & Co., 1925), which is an entertaining and often bizarre study of the prodigy Erwin Nyiregyházy, and which mentions an earlier von Hornbostel study of the compositional prodigy Korngold. (Some readers will remember the rediscovery of Nyiregyházy in Los Angeles in the 1970s and the resumption of his career as a pianist: it would appear that the qualifications for being a child prodigy included a future move to Hollywood.) One likewise recalls the fascination of Freud and the psychoanalytic circle with the artistic temperament, yet the central schools of psychology have always concentrated on common capacities.

point at which the new sciences escape the canon with some precision at the turn-of-the-century birth of the new discipline of comparative musicology, parented by a collaboration of historical musicology and musical psychology.

Schenker's handling of the canon, against those treatments ventured above, is all the more remarkable. His canon is a much more supple agency than it seems at first acquaintance. This is revealed by a comparison between the composer citations of *Harmony* and *Counterpoint* I and those of *Free Composition*. *Harmony* cites works of Johann Sebastian and Carl Philipp Emanuel Bach, Beethoven, Berlioz, Brahms, Bruckner, Chopin, Handel, Hassler, Haydn, Liszt, Mendelssohn, Mozart, Scarlatti, Schubert, Schumann, Richard Strauss, Sweelinck, and Wagner. The first volume of *Counterpoint* drops Berlioz, Hassler, Scarlatti, and Sweelinck and adds Graun, Wolf, Smetana, and Couperin. This roster changes tellingly, though, in *Free Composition*. Schenker adds single examples of Clementi, Crüger, Des Prez, and Paganini as well as multiple examples of the elder and younger Johann Strauss. Yet he omits the nineteenth-century modernists altogether from his new canon: Berlioz, Bruckner, Liszt, Smetana, Richard Strauss, and Wagner.

As the last two composers listed above take on a significant role in *Harmony* and *Counterpoint* I, their absence from *Free Composition* is particularly striking.[11] One might, again, most simply read a political subtext into this move and speak of how Schenker, the embittered monarchist of the post-war period, locating a cancer within the body of German musical culture (the New German school of composers) which will metastasize in the form of the modernist music of the Weimar republic, feels that he must figuratively excise this cancer. In extending this scenario, one might also speak of Schenker, as he conflates the technology of the new musical sciences with this modernism, reasserting the authority of the canon as an act of resistance against these sciences.

---

11 In *Harmony* Schenker is suprisingly charitable to Wagner and Strauss. After the war his position hardens, and by the time of *Free Composition* he clearly distinguishes between "idea" composers and those composers who understand (or more accurately understood) the power of diminution (pp. 26–27). Yet the analysis of Wagner's harmony stands as almost a benchmark for harmonic theorists in the latter half of the nineteenth and the first half of the twentieth century, and it would seem implausible for Schenker not to have had some familiarity with this literature. Nattiez makes an intriguing study of the various readings of the "Tristan chord" in a section entitled "Principles at Work in Constructing Harmonic Analysis" in *Music and Discourse* (pp. 216–223). We also cannot avoid noting that Georg Capellen begins his career with a monograph entitled *Ist das System S. Sechter's ein geeigneter Ausgangspunkt für die theoretische Wagnerforschung?* (Leipzig: C. F. Kahnt, 1902).

Plausible as this narrative is, the evidence admits a quite different reading. Schenker, to draw together the disparate strands of his discourse, locates a particular point of synthesis in the idealist formula that "the inner life of the tones" which stands outside of the epistemologies justifies these various strands. In order to render this formula useful, he is required to define this inner life in terms of a loosely specified body of works – a canon; and to deepen his epistemology, he is required, by compensation, to tighten his own version of the canon. Thus, it is in the closure of his canon that Schenker can claim (as he does repeatedly) to have constructed a supra-historical discourse while, in truth, only engaging a particular and highly qualified slice of the history of music, and it is also through this closure that he can claim to map a reception of music not predicated on the listener's occupying (if vicariously) the same historical moment as the composer, while he confines this reception to a historically defined body of texts. As powerful as is the case for closure as an ideological move, the case for closure as a logical or epistemological move, a way of making the various strands of his discourse commensurable, is equally powerful.

At each point at which there is a synthetic motion underlying Schenker's claims, one comes upon some sort of closure or limitation essential to this synthesis. Schenker can allow his politics a free rein inasmuch as he can claim his analysis to be anthropological (in that it describes a musical culture or matrix of assumptions held in common by the masters) and physiological (in that it rests on the assumption of a body of common perceptual mechanisms). Both terms of this opposition, however, are closed. He does not specify an anthropology which could apply to other bodies of work, and, likewise, his notion of perception, resting on an arbitrary (if fluid) hierarchy of musical materials such as pitch and rhythm and dynamics, disallows the perception of music which would manifest a different hierarchy. Similarly, he speaks of a compositional process, yet he restricts that process to specific individuals, and speaks of musical listening, while he allows it only to individuals who have learned to hear correctly.

This last point can be expanded. The musicologist presumes a transparency grounded in a musical culture shared between the composer and the contemporary audience, and the psychoacoustician presumes that the composer and the listener hold a certain musical capacity in common. Schenker gives a rather peculiar twist to this argument, addressing (through the agency of the closed canon) a problem of extension common to both the musicologist's and the psychologist's mediations of composer and listener. When examined in terms of this transaction, the task of musicology (both historic and comparative) involves not the reconciliation of culturally remote musics to the modern ear but the reconciliation of that ear to those musics. This, however, gives rise to a series of questions: Must an audience develop a distinct "ear" for each piece of music? Does this mean that the audience must conceive of music, as a whole, as an infinite collection of discrete hearings? Or should it hear each piece in terms of predecessors and successors, in terms of a historical process? Similarly, for the psychologist or the psychologistic theorist the musical event exists as a stimulus for a fixed mental processing. Does this mean, however, that there are certain events which lie beyond the musical hearing? Both series of questions prompt sometimes fruitful and sometimes simply peculiar lines of investigation (which would include the musical hermeneutics of the early twentieth century and the later notion of reception history).[12] But Schenker locates his theory outside of these problematics. In closing his canon and thus closing his analysis, Schenker at once substantiates and isolates what is to be taken as music, and thus avoids any problem of extension. Music, as such, is to be found only at that place where the historically correct moment and the psychologically defined space of composition and reception coincide.

12 In a sense, the whole notion of a musical symbol is an attempt to isolate some essence which supersedes both history and psychology, and thus anchors the musical experience regardless of variations in the audience. (This point is central to Schering's *Das Symbol in der Musik*.) The reception history accepts the historical variation of the audience, and hence fixes on the notion of multiple hearings. The musical work exists solely within an ever-changing "horizon of expectations." (The notion of reception history of course postdates Schenker significantly.) The psychological limits of music were of some concern early in the twentieth century (perhaps under the prompting of compositional evolutions). Otto Abraham and Karl Schaefer document some interesting experiments whose purpose is to elucidate the effect of speed on pitch perception in the article "Ueber die maximale Geschwindigkeit von Tonfolgen" in *Beiträge zur Akustik und Musikwissenschaft*, vol. III (1901), 13–21, and it is a standard strategy for empirical psychologists to test whether individuals with absolute pitch can name all of the constituent tones of a complex "atonal" sonority: see Stumpf, *Tonpsychologie* II, 369–370 and Révész, *The Psychology of a Musical Prodigy*, 77–83. (Considering the time, these "experiments" are fascinating.) The perception of temperament and substandard intervals are likewise engaged as a place at which the boundaries of music can be discerned. See the exchange between Max Arend's "Ist der Kreis der Konsonanzen nur historisch oder a priori geschlossen?" in *Neue Zeitschrift für Musik* 83 (1916), 165–167, and Ludwig Riemann's "Konsonanzgefühl und mathematische Akustik" in *Neue Zeitschrift für Musik* 83 (1916), 385–386. As one would suspect, there is evidence that the psychologists working on the perception of music had rather conservative musical tastes: see the close of Stumpf's "Differenztöne und Konsonanz" in *Beiträge zur Akustik und Musikwissenschaft* 6 (1911), 151–165. There is also a considerable contemporary literature attacking the music of Schoenberg through a consistently specious psychological reasoning.

REPRESENTATION

While we may be unable to define the notion of an epistemological synthesis, we would think of it as a motivation for the intricate series of moves whereby Schenker folds his various projects and various discourses together. We can also say that this synthesis involves a number of closures – first that of an objectification of the musical work or the assignment of a transcendental value to the musical text, then that of the identification of the transcendental text with the canon, and with the closure of the canon.

The connection between this move to a synthesis and Schenker's constructions respectively of a descriptive psychology and explanatory history, however, is not as intimate as we would like. Indeed, we might speak of synthesis as a motivation for these latter moves, yet it seems more a separate agenda, and we might still be troubled by a sense of contradiction between the idealist notion of synthesis and the qualified empiricism we have established in Schenker's project.

There is a particular way, though, in which one can uncover the evidence of a valid marriage between these agendas. As noted, in substituting synthesis for system in gathering up the various discursive strands of his earlier work, Schenker locates a place (given concrete shape as the canon) that stands outside of earlier attempts to determine a structure for musical studies as a whole. In doing so, though, he does not arrive at a representation of musical study in which each discourse assumes a parity and in which the claims of one against the other are subsumed in a mutual system of alliances. Rather, he arrives at a representation of musical study in which the empirical investigations of music are subordinated to his own master discourse. In other words, at the close of his work Schenker would accept an empirical musicology, yet he would stipulate that this musicology be framed in terms of his analysis, and he would accept a musical psychology with the same provision.[13]

One voice, of course, makes the same sort of claims. This is the voice of the music critic. Criticism, like Schenker's synthesis, conceives of itself as a discourse which stands over the empirical discourses of music,

---

13 By the time of *The Masterwork in Music*, Schenker has abandoned all overt references or appeals to the psychological sciences (which at this point would have been far removed from the sort of psychologies with which he might have been familiar in his younger days) and he of course only glancingly acknowledges systematic musicology. He does, however, claim priority over the philosophers and aestheticians (*Free Composition*, xxiv) and the music historians (*Free Composition*, 27): we might see these fields as displacements of psychology and systematic musicology.

appropriating the results of the musicologist's or theorist's work as it chooses in order to fashion interpretations or in order to come to grips with a reality unavailable to the epistemologically secure areas of musical study. Schenker, himself, is a critic, and he might easily see his later work returning to the same ideological or idealist grounds as did the critics of the early nineteenth century.

More accurately, though, Schenker's synthesis engages in a complex transaction with the discipline of music criticism. The key which unlocks the mechanics of this transaction is the notion of a closed canon. The canon to which Schenker holds and, in fact, the very idea, itself, of a canon is a legacy of the Romantic critics, specifically of their elevation of the transcendental figure of the master composer. Given the verbal excess of these critics, one might be excused for considering this move as no more than a product of the general Romantic ideology of such figures as Jean Paul and Wackenroder. As has been the case before, however, we stand to gain more of an insight by unpacking this notion epistemologically and by looking upon the figure of the transcendental composer (and, by extension, the canonic text) as a contingent solution to the same epistemological problems which would later prompt the creation of the new musical sciences of the later nineteenth century. In short, the eighteenth-century musical discourse contains the seed of the notion of the canon, but it has no clear conception of a distinct and transcendental college of master composers – it has no need of such. Music, in common with the other arts, is taken to be imitative, to represent discrete emotional states. Some composers would undoubtedly have more skill at such representations (hence the eighteenth-century conception of "genius"), yet every piece of music could be said to have a semantic content. Hence, one of the important and recurring projects of the eighteenth-century agenda involves the tabulation of the means whereby such imitations are to be most effectively rendered. For the Romantic critics and also for the major figures of critical philosophy who are interested in music such as Hegel and Schopenhauer, and for Hanslick, however, the very notion of representation has become problematic.[14] At the same moment that music is

---

14 Hanslick's formalist aesthetic is grounded in the rejection of any simple construal of representation. The critical investigations of Hegel and Schopenhauer are more interesting. For each, the question of the ontology of music turns on its peculiar capacity both to represent and to frustrate our attempts to define what is being represented and how this is accomplished. Hegel's aesthetic system is grounded in a sophisticated typology of representation. Music is located at the synthetic terminus of a motion from symbolic art (in which the phenomenal medium dominates the transcendental

understood to have an almost unchallenged capacity for expression, the meaning it conveys slips away, the tabulation of affects so important to the eighteenth-century aesthetician dissolves. Thus, the project of music criticism (at least in its more sophisticated manifestations) is born not from the examination of musical representations but from a radical critique of the very possibility of representation. Thus also the critic needs to bring into existence a figure who, without question, possesses this power of representation (which can be neither captured nor denied). The critic needs the canonic composer to restore some sense of balance to the musical world.

We would note, however, that for the critic the college of canonic composers and thus the collection of canonic works remains open (at least in potential) and that for many of the late nineteenth- and early twentieth-century critics the possibility of a musical hermeneutics, a decoding of musical meaning, remains likewise open. In other words, for a certain school of critics a lost repleteness seems, if not within reach, within conception. There are, on the other hand, those critics for whom a hermeneutics is not a convincing possibility. We would, without question, remember that (before Schenker) Hanslick moves beyond the composer and skeptically confronts the causal and experiential presumptions of musical representation, and, by contrast, remember that even Adorno (after Schenker), a critic who, in his proposed sociology of music, is deeply committed to the question of the construction of musical meaning, insists on the autonomy and internal logic of the creative process and the musical work.[15] Representation thus remains the central problem of musical criticism.

<hr/>

idea, and which is best exemplified in Oriental art) through the "classical" arts (in which the medium and the idea are brought into balance, as in the Hellenic arts) to the "romantic" arts (in which the idea dominates the medium). Music constitutes the most romantic of the arts in that its medium can only be defined as an absence, a double negation of space and substance. See *Aesthetics: Lectures on Fine Arts*, trans. T. M. Knox (Oxford: Clarendon Press, 1975), vol. II, 888–958. Likewise, Schopenhauer defines music as a negation inasmuch as the contemplation of music is the only occasion on which perception is not animated or contaminated by the transcendental ideas which mediate between the noumenal "Will" and the phenomenal world. It is only by virtue of the disinterested (or "will-less") nature of this perceptual moment that one is in music permitted an unadulterated glimpse of reality. Thus music represents, yet does so in a way which has no corollaries in the other arts. See *The World as Will and Idea*, I, §52, II, §39; trans. R. B. Haldane and J. Kemp (London: Kegan Paul, Trench, Trübner & Co., 1896; rpt. New York: AMS Press, 1977), vol. I, 330–346; vol. III, 231–244.

15 Adorno in particular is extremely sensitive to the problem of representation: he needs some such notion in order to validate his sociology, yet is wary of any too-simple reading of social structures

While he may aim to recover the same repleteness within his synthesis, Schenker goes about this task in quite an opposite manner. Certainly, his canon will not admit new texts. And even beyond this we might go so far as to venture that his synthesis does not truly inscribe the composer as a transcendental agent. He speaks with reverence of the canonic master, yet the true object of his study is strictly confined to the body of texts themselves. The human figure of the composer, that historical being whose desires and intentions and situations give meaning to the musical work, is abstracted as a generalized historical and psychological moment. He has no personal history, no development – even within the works themselves.

The transcendental figure at the center of Schenker's synthesis is thus closed in the sense that it exists only in the concrete form of a collection of musical texts. By extension, the mechanics of representation is also closed. Representations of music cannot be arrived at by the reconstruction of the composer or the act of composition, they can only be approached through the agency of other representations. One can speak of the musical text only in terms of other musical texts, fix the musical meaning only through other musical meanings.

In line with our earlier notion of Schenker's synthesis (as a binding together of different discursive strands) we might extend this notion to cover music criticism. We would venture that various essays constitute a critical project over the course of his career, and that *Free Composition* stands as a formalized critical theory with his analysis constituting a sort of displaced critical practice. There is some truth to this assertion, but there is a deeper truth available to us. Inasmuch as Schenker closes the notion of representation by stipulating that music can only be represented by other music and thus, conversely, that music may only represent other music, he can be said to dissolve (at least within the domain of his synthesis) the problem that lies at the theoretical heart of music criticism. Hence, we

into music. For example, we read in his *Introduction to the Sociology of Music*, trans. E. B. Ashton (New York: Seabury Press, 1976), 215: "It is true that the problems and solutions of works of art do not arise beyond the systems of social norms. But they do not acquire social dignity until they remove themselves from those norms; the highest productions actually negate them. The esthetic quality of works, their truth content, has little to do with any truth that can be empirically pictured, not even with the life of the soul. But it converges with social truth. It is more than the mere conceptless appearance of the social process in the works, although it is always that too. As a totality, each work takes a position on society and by its synthesis anticipates reconcilement. The organized aspect of works is borrowed from social organization; they transcend that in their protest against the principle of organization itself, against dominion over internal and external nature."

might more accurately assert that by this move, he does not subsume but rather completely rewrites the critical agenda.[16]

This move rather obviously weds Schenker's synthetic argument to his epistemological agendas. In closing the possibility of musical representation in on itself he also closes the possibilities of both a psychological analysis and a historical description that need to stand (through a symbolic system or through a narrative) outside of the notation itself. But Schenker's reinscription of criticism and his historical and psychological projects are bound more profoundly. While we would assert that Schenker closes the problem of musical representation, we cannot assert that he denies the notion of musical meaning. Quite on the contrary, as we have noted, he unpacks this synthesis in terms of an extravagant accumulation of social and political pronouncements, he puts forward an explicitly ideological reading of the meaning of music. Indeed, one might plausibly read the notion of synthesis itself not as a logical but as an ideological move. Yet what is interesting here is the question of ordering. We may accept, for the sake of argument, the assertion that the meaning of a musical text is political or social. But we would expect this meaning to be argued as a product of such

16 This is an abstract and difficult argument, involving, as it does, the displacement of Schenker's theory onto the field of criticism. We might say that replacement of traditional criticism by Schenker's analysis mirrors his historical narrative, which takes the turn from vocal composition to instrumental composition as a decisive liberation from the enslavement of tones to the word. One point which is interesting, and which may be suggestive in regard to the doubling over of representation, is a sudden problematization of the notion of "hearing" after the First World War. (Riemann has of course always written about the notion of "hearing", and Schering is the author of a pre-war text entitled *Musikalische Bildung und Erziehung zum musikalischen Hören* [Leipzig: Quelle & Meyer, 1911; 4th edn. 1924], but the feel of the post-war readings is different.) For example, we have Gustav Becking, "'Hören' und 'Analysieren'" in *Zeitschrift für Musikwissenschaft* 1 (1919), 587–603. A rather interesting notion of "form-hearing" (and another analysis of the C minor fugue) is advanced by Rudolf Steglich in "Das c moll-Präludium aus dem ersten Teil des Wohltemperierten Klaviers J. S. Bachs" in the *Bach Jahrbuch* 20 (1923), 1–11. The problem of hearing and the notion of atonality is dealt with in Lotte Kallenbach's "Das musikalische Hören" in *Die Musik* 17/4 (January 1925), 271–278. Certainly the notion of a problematized hearing is central to Schenker's developed thought. This new emphasis may in some part result from the shift in the psychological paradigm. We can perhaps relate it to the broader construction of experiential evidence central to the thinking of the post-Wundt structural psychologists, or (as suggested by the Kallenbach article) to the appearance of a new and challenging music. Yet one might prefer to relate this emphasis on hearing to a local opposition developing between the hermeneutic readings of Kretzschmar and Schering, which solve the problem of representation by locating an explicit textual content in the music, and the analytic readings of the theorists. Intriguingly enough, a more radical aesthetician, arguing for a "phenomenology" of music, sees Schenker (in concert with August Halm and Hans Pfitzner) putting forward an outdated hermeneutics: see Paul Bekker, "Was ist Phänomenologie der Musik?" in *Die Musik* 17/4 (January, 1925), 241–249.

extra-textual considerations. Schenker, by contrast, ventures the reverse, rhetorically situating his examination of music anterior to his ideology, arguing, as he would have it, his political agenda as a product of his analysis of music. The reason for this may be pragmatic in part. Schenker, unlike those critics of the political left, does not have what we might call a coherent and ramified political analysis to map onto the musical text. (This, in fact, may be one reason why we can so easily disentangle his analysis from his political and social views.) Whatever the motivation, this move entails the isolation or closure of his analysis. But it also involves a sort of closure of his epistemological agenda. We might conceive of Schenker attempting to validate his ideology through the appropriation of, let us say, the work of the narrative historian or the work of the developmental psychologist rather than that of the paleographer or the textual critic or the psycho-acoustician. Instead, he turns to precisely those areas of musicology and musical psychology most empirical and in practice most insulated from any interpretive attribution of meaning. Thus, in its motivation and in its particulars, his epistemological synthesis involves the same sort of closure as his erasure of the critical agenda.

A PRIORI AND A POSTERIORI THEORIES

The above line of thought leads us into a somewhat difficult position. We have rather loosely named various discursive strands such as "musicology," "musical psychology," "music theory," and "music criticism." We need not be concerned, in particular, with defining the first two of these studies, but having defined "music criticism" in terms of the problematics of the notion of musical representation and musical meaning, we might be tempted to define theory as a study that (like criticism) is in origin neither historiological nor psychological, yet one that forecloses the question of musical meaning (rather than problematizing it). In other words, the project of the critic turns on the mechanics of musical semantics and the project of the theorist turns on the mechanics of musical syntax. We would have to acknowledge, however, that this formula is too simple. Schenker is a theorist, after all. Yet his theory does not stand in opposition to the critical agenda but rather subsumes that agenda. Our received notion of a distinction between criticism and theory, or even between these projects and the more empirical studies of music, would thus seem inadequate.

Perhaps it is necessary to reconceive the pattern of relations holding between these various ways of speaking of music. To this end, we might appropriate the representation of the discursive economies of the human sciences given by Michel Foucault. In brief, Foucault proposes an "archeology" of the ways in which life, language, and economic exchange are treated historically. He claims to uncover a series of epistemological structures (Renaissance, Classical, and Modern) within which these various subjects are uniquely disposed as sciences. He further makes the point that none of these three systems maps onto another, and that the sciences peculiar to one system do not develop into the sciences of the next but instead are catastrophically displaced.[17] In particular, he locates the origins of the modern epistemological system in the sudden appearance, at the close of the eighteenth century, of a distinction between things–in–themselves and their phenomenal appearances, a distinction (as we well recall) first articulated clearly in Kant's critical philosophy, in which the crisis of classical theories of knowledge is addressed through the postulation of transcendental agencies which stand before perception or consciousness. But it is evidenced most clearly in the formation of four distinct epistemologies or discursive modes consistent within each of the human sciences. The first takes form in that place occupied (as in Kant's epistemology) by the *a priori* transcendental. In particular, this is the place where life or language or labor is studied in terms of formal systems and the like that are taken to govern phenomenal appearances. The second of these epistemologies takes form in that place where life or language or labor take on a presence (as may be the case in Schopenhauer's science). It is the place of the *a posteriori* transcendental that itself is taken to govern phenomenal

---

17 Foucault arrays the human sciences of the seventeenth and eighteenth centuries (the analysis of wealth, natural history, general grammar) according to four representational functions which between them form a table – attribution, articulation, designation, and derivation. Into this table are introduced at the close of the eighteenth century three concepts (labor, organic structure, inflectional systems) which undermine these respective sciences and in short order give rise to the different sciences of economics, biology, and philology which are themselves disposed between and beneath the four points of the classical table. We might speak of a Classical theory of music (disposed among whole–number acoustics, harmony, the classification of affects, and the codification of musical rhetoric) being displaced by a Modern musicology. (See in particular Foucault's table, *The Order of Things*, 201.) My reading of nineteenth-century musical studies departs from Foucault's reading in the place he assigns to the idealist historiography of the time. Although there is a strain of such historiography in music, complete with discussions of historical epochs and ideal types and the like, and although it would be fascinating to delve into the covering laws of these narratives, historical narratives (in this sense) play a small role in modern musicology. But we should bear in mind that Schenker himself distinguishes historical narrative from historical research. I think that the place of these idealistic histories has been most interestingly filled in our own discourse by political and gender readings of the history of music and its texts.

appearances. Thus, in the domain of the transcendental there arises an epistemological counterpoint of (again in Foucault's usage) the "subjective analysis" and the "objective synthesis."[18] Against this symmetry there forms a second wherein the internal laws of phenomenal appearances themselves are the subject of examination. This is the domain of the empirical sciences (which for each term manifest themselves in two distinct sciences).[19]

Foucault puts forward an intricately ramified theory to which we cannot do justice in such a brief space. We can, however, give his analysis both a bit more depth and a relevance by transposing it upon the various musical discourses arising in the second half of the nineteenth century. Foucault's epistemological structure can be conceived as a square outside of each of whose sides lies a particular discursive field. Beyond two opposing sides lie the domains of the empirical disciplines – in this case, the sciences of musicology and the sciences of the psychology of music. The first has at its core the assumption that there exist in written documents internal laws governing the representation of music which can be apprehended empirically. The second has at its core the notion that perception is likewise governed by empirically available laws or mental structures. From these respective investigations the notions of a history and of a psychology of music take on concrete substance, and around them are arrayed subsidiary disciplines: archival and biographical studies, organology, comparative musicology, the psychology of reception, the investigation of the musically precocious or gifted. (Foucault himself would project the figure of the quadrilateral into three dimensions – give it five faces and dispose these various disciplines downward from the upper face according to their increasing degree of empiricity. Inasmuch as the reason for this has to do with the way in which his Modern discursive structure displaces its Classical predecessor, we need not factor it into our reading.) Beyond the other two sides lie the respective fields of the transcendental *a priori* and the transcendental *a posteriori*, the subjective analysis and the objective synthesis.

18 See *The Order of Things*, 243–249.

19 These empirical doubles for the nineteenth-century sciences include (for language) phonetics and syntax, (for biology) comparative anatomy and physiology, and (for economics) the analysis of production and the analysis of distribution. The corresponding double for musicology is (of course) the complex of paleography and textual criticism on the one hand and the complex of physiological acoustics and the empirical investigation of perception on the other. Perhaps the first indications we have of this new empirical double are found at the close of the eighteenth century in Ernst Chladni's *Entdeckung über die Theorie des Klangs* (Leipzig: Weidmann, 1787) and Martin Gerbert's *Scriptores ecclesiastici de musica sacra potissimum* (St. Blasien, 1784) – both of which, most interestingly, are published at about the same time as the first stirrings of a musical Romanticism.

It would appear obvious that those modes of writing that we would think of as music theory and music criticism are disposed in these latter two fields. It would not be out of place to assign, provisionally, theory to the field of the *a priori* and criticism to the field of the *a posteriori*. Yet Schenker draws us up short, forces us to question not simply this assignment but more our conception of an opposition between theory and criticism. Schenker's late theory, with its assignment of a transcendental presence to the canon and with its peculiar awareness of musical psychology and history, situates itself with ease in the domain of the objective synthesis. Therein are we forced to consider a rather different opposition, one which divides theory itself into two broad areas and one which may do the same with criticism.

In extension, working from the above-mentioned thought, we might as a sort of experiment wish to extrapolate what sort of discourse would, perchance, lie across from that of Schenker. It would be a discourse that situates itself before rather than after the investigations of the phenomenal appearances of music. It would be presumptively unaware of notation and perception, or in other words, insensitive to the internal laws governing these phenomena. Thus, it would be a discourse in which one would not think to construct the composer or the canon as transcendental subjects. Furthermore, in placing itself outside of history and refusing to assign a transcendental presence to the canonic composer or text, it would lend itself more easily to the practice of composition. Finally, looking to discover that which transpires before the psychological and cultural experiences of music, while conscious of the necessity to justify itself epistemologically against the empirical claims of the sciences of these receptions, it would find its voice in a language consistent, coherent, and semantically transparent (looking at some point toward these qualities in a mathematics or logic).

This extrapolation may be over-clever, yet within it we gain some approximation of the nature of this new symmetry and (as a bonus) begin to situate Schenker in a larger context. It goes almost without saying that the discourse characterized above is in most respects identical to that of the familiar school of theory which, appealing to the extensive development of formal logic and epistemology and the theorization of scientific method, comes into being in the second half of the twentieth century.[20] (It is not

---

20 Specifically (or parochially) I think of the circle of theorists gathered around Milton Babbitt in the 1960s. The manifesto for this circle would have to be Babbitt's "The Structure and Function of Music Theory" [1965] in *Perspectives on Contemporary Music Theory*, ed. Benjamin Boretz and Edward Cone (New York, Norton, 1972), 10–21, wherein he calls for a music theory that can hold its own against the empirical authority of other disciplines through a scrupulous attention to language and

unreasonable to imagine that this notion of theory has antecedents reaching far back into the eighteenth century. One is immediately reminded of Hauptmann's appropriation of the logic of the Hegelian dialectic and of Riemann's dualist harmony as evidence of an implicit notion of an autonomous musical logic. With regard to this last example, it is interesting to note the compositional appearance of symmetrical pitch structures occurring at practically the exact moment at which physiological acoustics and the literature of music theory postulate a harmonic symmetry.)[21] Both this analytic theory and Schenker's synthesis concern themselves with the manipulation of pitch structures, yet rather than taking them as a single project, we would more accurately see them as counter-theories.

But this formula is almost too convenient, and Foucault's structure may be better understood if we jog this school of formalist theory and Schenker's synthesis from their easy symmetry. As noted, Foucault thinks of each of the four discursive locations not as points but as fields or domains which contain a variety of different discourses arrayed, at times, by degree of empiricism, at times by differing constructions of the subject. Such can

a deep and continuing epistemological reflection. Boretz and Cone's introduction to this volume gives a fascinating account of the range of projects available to this group of theorists (ibid., vii–x), and in particular contrasts their relativism (both mild and radical) with the universalism of earlier theorists. One work stands at the apogee of attempts to construct a radically relative theory: see Benjamin Boretz, "Meta-variations: Studies in the Foundations of Musical Thought, Part I: Thought (I)," *Perspectives of New Music* 8/1 (Fall–Winter 1969), 1–74; "Part II: Sketch of a Musical System," *Perspectives of New Music* 8/2 (Spring–Summer 1970), 23–48; "Meta-variations, Part III: The Construction of a Musical Syntax (I)," *Perspectives of New Music* 9/1 (Fall–Winter 1970), 23–42; "Musical Syntax (II)," *Perspectives of New Music* 9/2–10/1 (Spring–Summer–Fall–Winter 1971), 232–270; "Meta-variations Part IV: Analytic Fallout (I)," *Perspectives of New Music* 11/1 (Fall–Winter 1972), 146–223; "Analytic Fallout (II)," *Perspectives of New Music* 11/2 (Spring–Summer 1973), 156–203. The reading which best captures the distinction between different theories (in addition to noting the ties which bind Schenker's analysis to performance theory and the historiographic conception) is Michael Mann, "Schenker's Contribution to Music Theory" in the *Music Review* 10 (1949), 3–26. Interestingly, Mann conceives Schenker's analysis as an *a posteriori* artifact (inasmuch as it involves a closed canon).

21 We have good reason to read any encounters between music theory (or the musical discourse as a whole) and composition very cautiously. We simply note the temporal coincidence of Helmholtz's postulation of an undertone series and Riemann's harmonic dualism with the occasional exact symmetry found in Wagner (as in the opening of *Tristan und Isolde* and the opening of the third act of *Parsifal*). In this instance, I think the most powerful argument for some sophisticated symmetrical "pre-compositional" thinking in Wagner is put forward in Benjamin Boretz's provocatively counterintuitive reading of the opening of *Tristan* in "Meta-variations, Part IV: Analytic Fallout (I)," 159–217. Again, Nattiez makes an intriguing case for the interaction of theory (specifically harmonic theory) and composition in a section entitled "Semiology of Harmonic Theories and Harmonic Practices" in *Music and Discourse* (212–216).

be seen in the empirical fields where once (in our case) the history of music becomes internally demonstrable, a whole collection of other studies are authorized or reauthorized; where once the mechanics of perception becomes available to quantitative and qualitative measure, an extended notion of the musical psychology becomes (in potential) viable. We would allow this same breadth or complexity to those domains in which fall theory and criticism.

In regard to the characterization of modern formalized theory, four points need to be stressed. This mode of discourse takes shape as a theory that is, in a loose sense, compositional (in that it is not tied to a fixed and transcendental composer or canon). It is discursively autonomous (in that its argument stands outside of history or psychology). It is consistent (in that it is epistemologically self-aware) and it is transparent (in that the statements it makes about music need in some way to be verifiable). By our earlier logic, we might characterize Schenker's theory as interpretive, inclusive, experiential (in that it relies on the integrity of its report of musical experience instead of on internal coherence), and linguistically problematic. With this last point we have difficulty. As noted previously, Schenker's synthesis is predicated on dissolving what can be taken as a linguistic dilemma: he can speak of psychology and of history simultaneously only by subsuming them in the same meta-language, by turning music as a representation on itself, using it to represent itself. It would seem thus that he also predicates his analysis on a transparency of language. Following this, a true counter-discourse to that of Schenker would be, as it was before, compositional, autonomous, and consistent. Yet it would also problematize (or even re-problematicize) language. In fact, we might speculate that it would mirror Schenker's move, that where Schenker would arrive at a representational transparency in using music as a language or symbol system with which to speak of music, it would take the language used to speak of music as itself a music.[22]

---

22 I think specifically (and again parochially) of the later work of James Randall and Benjamin Boretz. See, for example, James Randall, "how music goes" in *Perspectives of New Music* 14/2, 15/1 (Spring–Summer–Fall–Winter 1976), 424–497, and Benjamin Boretz, "Language, as a Music" in *Perspectives of New Music* 17/2 (Spring–Summer 1979), 131–196. See also, for a slightly different take, Marjorie Tichenor, "Getting to gnaw all about you" in *Perspectives of New Music* 20/1 (Fall–Winter 1981, Spring–Summer, 1982), 406–412, and John Cage, "Sculpture Musicale" in *Perspectives of New Music* 26/1 (Winter, 1988), 12–25. It is easy to see a disjunction between this material and the earlier epistemologically-rigorous work of the former pair of authors. But the differences of surface conceal a very interesting move. Where the epistemologically rigorous theorist (such as Babbitt or the early Boretz) will claim that the very transparency and efficiency of his theoretical language

If we open the field of the *a priori* to such seemingly opposing projects, we open the field of the *a posteriori* likewise. This allows a clarification of an earlier point. Again, a true complement to the formalized discourse of the theorist would be interpretive, inclusive, experiential, and linguistically problematic. This description would apply to many of the projects assigned to the genre of music criticism. Where it seemed important, earlier, to draw a distinction between these projects and Schenker's, now, with more sophistication, we might look to what holds them together. When we come to locate Schenker's synthesis within the discursive domain of the transcendental *a posteriori*, we see, in fact, that it occupies a place within a very complex community of real and possible discourses, some of which reach beyond the music to idealize the composer, some of which, at times, appeal to transcendental constructions such as style or genre, and many of which admit complex systems of transcendentals.

Yet before this is done, we need to establish a different characterization of our various discourses. If some transaction between Schenker and the critic is to be substantiated, we must be careful not to retrace our steps to an easy identification of music theory with the *a priori* and music criticism with the *a posteriori*, or even to qualify this identification (by saying that the field of the *a priori* contains a formalized theory and a radical variant, and

cannot but render any distinction between thinking about music and producing music meaningless, these theorists, taking language as something itself opaque, will deny that we can use language to speak of music without that language in some way becoming a music. To approach this motion another way, the theoretical project of Babbitt and the early Boretz grows out of a rigorous epistemological hygiene. The epistemology of these theorists is, however, to borrow a distinction from Quine, "conceptual" rather than "doctrinal." It concerns itself with meaning (which is determined by context) rather than with truth (which lies within the domain of the natural sciences). In other words, the logically sensitive analyst constructs a reading of a musical text in which particular statements are corrigible only in terms of the passage itself, in which no statement can rely on the analyst's feeling or previous knowledge. Thus, the analysis cannot assert any general truth about musical experience but can claim only to show what particular events mean within the context of the entire text. We might hypothesize a "crisis" in music theory in the late 1970s in which this conceptual epistemology loses its authority, a crisis which admits two solutions, the first a turn (or return) to a naturalized epistemology (signalled by the appearance of the new journal *Music Perception*) and the second an abandonment of the forms and authority of the scientific method in favor of a more radical construction of contextual meaning or musical behavior. See Willard Quine, "Epistemology Naturalized" in *Ontological Relativity and Other Essays* (New York, Columbia University Press, 1969), 69–90. A different but interesting reading of this move is found in Fred Maus, "Recent Ideas and Activities of James K. Randall and Benjamin Boretz: A New Social Role for Music," in *Perspectives of New Music* 26/2 (Summer, 1988), 214–222. The work of the "language as a music" theorists, and the motion it embodies, may seem very far afield from that of Schenker, yet it constitutes perhaps the clearest example of the problem of representation within a strictly "theoretic" discourse.

the field of the *a posteriori* music criticism and Schenker's variant of it).The field of the *a priori* may be further opened by locating in it, for example, an examination of music that is (in accord with our earlier criteria) autonomous and transparent, that nevertheless eschews a formal consistency and is, by compensation, radically experiential. One imagines here a phenomenological or even an existential reading of music claiming to establish an experience prior to perception or cultural processing, whose results, in some way, come to resemble what we might think of as criticism. We could also open the field of the *a posteriori* further, locating within it examinations of music not directly experiential, but relying on the analysis of the repleteness of experience. One can imagine here that sort of political criticism in which experience is taken to be the product of a collection of social or economic transactions and which can thus be justifiably said to be theoretical. Any distinction we would make between music theory and music criticism based on claims to abstraction or theorization is therefore invalid. The fields of the subjective analysis and the objective synthesis potentially dispose of discourses of varying degrees of abstract theorization in the same way that the fields of historical and comparative musicology and of musical psychology dispose of investigations of differing degrees of empiricism. Thus, while we might use these terms for convenience, we gain less purchase dividing the domain of the transcendental between music theory and music criticism than between a variously theorized *a priori* and a likewise variously theorized *a posteriori*.

TWO POLEMICS

One further point needs to be taken into account. To clarify matters, it would be most profitable to make explicit an assumption that has covertly crept into this last section of the argument. In making the case for Schenker's engagement with the empirical studies of music history and musical psychology, our argument was loosely historic, or, better, we might say it was genetic. In each case we located a crisis within the respective notions of music history and musical psychology whose solution gave rise to one sense of Schenker's mature analysis. On the other hand, in appropriating Foucault's epistemological structuralism (or, better, a portion of this structuralism) we abandoned, in large part, all but the vestiges of a historical argument. Foucault constructs each epistemological system as a structure not of discourses but of discursive possibilities. In other words, while, in the first section of this essay, we allowed ourselves a limited intertextuality, bringing, for example, Schenker and Dilthey into proximity without attempting to demonstrate that the former was (even) aware of the latter, Foucault now asks us to accept a radical intertextuality. He asks us, for example, to bring Schenker into proximity with such temporally removed figures as the "language as music" theorists or modern political critics.

We need not be overly concerned by this move, however. Realistically, to speak of Schenker in any theoretically substantive way is to speak of a series of receptions of Schenker, and even, if one is honest, to speak of his work as a continuing agent in our own discourse. A slightly different line of inquiry thus becomes available. Holding Foucault's analysis in mind as an interpretive tool, we may look to some of these receptions to do the work of situating Schenker's synthesis. In fact, to define this program further we might take a leaf from our own reading of Schenker wherein we first looked to those places – prefaces and introductions – in which Schenker himself felt it necessary to situate his agenda against a wider discourse, and to look not to explications of Schenker, but to those polemics wherein Schenker is brought into contact with (or held to task by) this author's own project.

One point which recurs in several of these polemics needs to be taken care of immediately. Schenker is on occasion accused of reducing the rich surface of the musical text to the static structure of the *Ursatz*.[23] The characterization of the *Ursatz* as static we can dismiss out of hand, but the notion of reduction is of more concern. In various respects we have already countered this critique. Schenker never speaks of his analysis as a reduction. As noted, his treatment of simultaneity and succession in the first volume of *Counterpoint* in fact sets us on a different path in that events are most likely seen as condensations of complexes of underlying operations. (For example, he explains a series of imperfect thirds and the psychological content

---

23 For example, Charles Rosen: "his method takes the form of a gradual reduction of the surface of the music to his basic phrase [the *Ursatz*], and the analysis moves in one direction, away from what is actually heard and toward a form which is more or less the same for every work. It is a method which, for all it reveals, concentrates on a single aspect of music and, above all, makes it impossible to bring the other aspects into play. The work appears to drain away into the secret form hidden within itself" ("Art Has its Reasons," *New York Review of Books* [17 June, 1971]: 38; quoted in Joseph Kerman, *Contemplating Music* [Cambridge, Mass.: Harvard University Press, 1985], 84). Again, we would assert that reduction (taken in even a trivial sense) is a much more complex operation than Rosen would admit: so complex, even, that Schenker himself speaks only guardedly of the successive elimination of diminution according to the procedures taught in certain textbooks (*Free Composition*, 26).

of the fourth in just this way.) Likewise, in a rather different way, his treatment of Bach's fugue subject, while predicated on the economy of a particular third-span, develops this span so elaborately as to make the actual text of the fugue subject a condensation of a complex matrix of background dynamics. Thus, when we come to the analysis of *Free Composition*, we are justifiably wary of the notion of reduction. One finds fewer events in any particular stratum than in its successor, and more than in its predecessor. Yet to look on an example of Schenker's analyses in this manner is to mistake one thing (the analytic notation) for another (the notation of the text). The important move in his analysis is not that between succeeding strata and surface, but between the aggregate of strata (taken as a single entity) and the surface. Hence, even if going by the gross criterion of the number of notational events, comparison of the number of notational things in the analysis as a whole with the number of notational things in the text renders the notion of reduction suspicious. If we go beyond this, if we accept the notion of the analytic strata as a recapitulation of a history of music, we are required to confirm our suspicions of the notion of reduction and instead see the surface of the text as a condensation of these historical forces. In other words, Schenker asks us to see history not as a smooth progression (although the analytic strata themselves, by convention, embody this feature) but as a disjunction. He asks us to hear in the complex of strata which make up the analysis a history that is for the most part hidden yet that becomes phenomenally available at the point where the accumulation of interior performances precipitates in the notation of the masters.

It could be argued that we have labored this point, that while the notion of reduction implies a sort of impoverishment, the assertions of the reductionists can be turned simply by introducing the complement of reduction: elaboration. To counter the picture of a reductive impoverishment of a rich musical surface, we might propose a picture of the analysis as the elaborative enrichment of a simple figure culminating in this same musical surface. In effect, we might counter a "bottom-up" reading with a "top-down" reading, and in doing so counter the notion of analysis as a process with the notion of analysis as a product. The conception of an elaborative analysis, though, fails for the same reason as did the conception of a reductive analysis. Schenker glories in elaboration and invention and embellishment, yet again he assigns to them a particular historical moment – the moment of diminution – and again, we must, ourselves, confine them to that place wherein the analysis crosses from interior performance to surface.

Although this distinction between a process of reduction or elaboration and a moment of condensation may seem a matter of local interpretation, it is important that we hold it in mind when we move to two ambitious polemics which, to our advantage, strongly position Schenker against a breadth of theories and critical projects, and which not uncoincidentally triangulate the American reception of Schenker. The first of these is Allen Forte's justly famous "Schenker's Conception of Musical Structure."[24] Forte's explication of Schenker's analysis (which, supplemented by his later textbook, we might now think of as the "standard model") stands on its own merits.[25] Of more immediate interest is the agenda that he draws up as a young and optimistic theorist for the future of Schenkerian studies. Forte puts forward five extensions of Schenker's project: (1) the construction of a theory of rhythm for tonal music, (2) the determination of the sources and development of triadic tonality, (3) the investigation of compositional technique and process, (4) the improvement of theory instruction, and (5) the application of the analysis to twentieth-century music. Even in retrospect we are impressed by his scope and ambition. In effect, having come across a powerful and potentially paradigmatic analysis, he maps a takeover of large sections of the musical discourse. Thus his program is of even more interest in that it is part of a larger institutional agenda, part of an attempt to establish music theory as an important and independent player among the various musical discourses of the academy.[26]

The second polemic postdates that of Forte by approximately twenty years. This is the critique of Schenker contained in Joseph Kerman's equally noted *Contemplating Music*.[27] If anything, the breadth of Kerman's agenda is more explicit. He undertakes a survey of the entirety of musical

---

24 Allen Forte, "Schenker's Conception of Musical Structure," *Journal of Music Theory* 3 (1959), 1–30. The term "structure" constitutes a strange semantic nexus. On the one hand, it refers back to a peculiarly Anglo-American usage in music theory (a usage exploited in Salzer's pioneering English-language treatment of Schenker) and on the other it pays homage to Carnap and the Vienna Circle (this homage being more apparent in Babbitt's "Structure and Function"). Then again, we might even go back to the "structural" psychologists. Schenker, to the best of my knowledge, never uses a German cognate for the term "musical structure."

25 See Allen Forte and Steven E. Gilbert, *Introduction to Schenkerian Analysis* (New York and London: W. W. Norton, 1982).

26 An overview of the move towards the institutional autonomy of music theory is found in Richmond Browne's "The Inception of the Society for Music Theory" in *Music Theory Spectrum*, 1 (1979), 2–5.

27 Kerman, *Contemplating Music*, pp. 82–84 for the discussion specifically of Forte's program, pp. 60–112 for the entire chapter on theory and analysis. Kerman's critique of the field will still (after ten years) touch some nerves, yet, perhaps for this very reason, should not be ignored.

investigation – music theory, musicology, ethnomusicology, perceptual studies, the authentic performance movement – all the while advancing his own case against the dominance within the musical discourse of an alienating positivist methodology. Schenker, in person, appears as the most prestigious purveyor of what Kerman terms the "formalist analysis," which he sees as having wrongly displaced "traditionalist criticism."

In any contest between these two polemics Kerman, having the advantage of hindsight, must come out ahead. Indeed, he carefully lays out Forte's agenda and grades its points one by one on their apparent success in the twenty-odd years following its publication. On one count – (4) the improvement of theory instruction – he concedes Forte's program a certain success. On all other counts, however, he judges Forte's agenda a failure. Kerman argues that this string of failures derives inevitably from the inadequacies of Schenker's analysis (and "formalist analysis" as a whole). Conceding his evaluation, we can explicate these failures rather differently, understand them as deriving not from some disabling flaw to be found in Schenker's work itself but rather from the very act of Forte's extension.

Forte proposes (1) the construction of a theory of rhythm for tonal music. Kerman rather lightly dismisses the subsequent attempts to construct such a theory by associating them with the several questionable postwar efforts to serialize rhythm or duration compositionally. The failure to define a paradigmatic theory of rhythm, however, deserves a rather different consideration. We would argue against a rhythmic theory that claims to situate itself within Schenker's synthesis on the grounds that the historical component of this representation locates the formation of rhythm precisely at that point wherein the body of interior performances condenses into an instrumental notation. This is not to rule out a theory of rhythm, but rather to rule out any theoretical system predicated on a logical coincidence of pitch and rhythm. In fact, we might speculate that a successful theory of rhythm, in order to correspond with Schenker's synthesis, would need to assign a priority to rhythm, isolating it, perhaps, as a descriptive procedure and joining it to some historical construction, and only then introducing pitch as a surface phenomenon.

Forte next proposes (2) an examination of the formation of tonality within the Schenkerian framework. If we concede Schenker's construction as a definition of something called "tonality," this proposal has an immediate logic, one which Schenker himself seems to endorse at some points. It fails, though, on somewhat the same grounds as the previous proposal.

Schenker's synthesis itself contains a history and to turn this account back on the formation of tonality is merely to reconfirm what is presumed already. The underlying strata of the analysis may strike us as "tonal," yet inasmuch as they are not themselves "music" but only notational representations of historical and psychological dynamics within a music, this appearance is a convention rather than a substantive quality. Tonality, like rhythm, comes into being at the moment when these dynamics are precipitated in the form of the notation of the masters.

Kerman handles the third point on Forte's agenda – (3) the investigation of compositional technique and process – more delicately. He obviously does not wish to discredit sketch studies as a whole in his evaluation and this is an area in which Forte has made an impressive personal investment: therefore his criticism is muted.[28] We ourselves cannot be as reticent. Schenker is interested in composer's autographs, yet he also cautions against reading the particular analytic applications of his theory as reports of the compositional development of the particular text (let alone as evidence of a generalized compositional method). Arguing (as we do) that the analysis of a particular text reconstructs one branch of the abstract and idealized history embodied in Schenker's synthesis makes us suspicious of the conception of the analysis as in any way embodying a concrete and particular history. To use Schenker's theory as a gauge against which to study a composer's methods or conception is to over-psychologize his theory at the expense of its historical component. Also, although Schenker often speaks intensely of the composer, this composer, as a complex individual with a personal history and with intention and individuality, seems not to have a true existence in his world, seems to stand outside of the synthesis. Thus, there is almost a moral dilemma intrinsic in Forte's project. One hesitates to draw out the point, yet in bringing sketch studies under the aegis of Schenker's method Forte, in effect, would subsume a most personal and particular investigation of the composer within a reading in which that same composer can have no substance except as a product of great psychological and historical forces.

---

28 In contrast to his disdain for most of the tasks of traditional musicology, Schenker himself speaks fervently of the importance of composers' autographs – which we have discussed in the second section of this work (*Free Composition*, 7). Forte, of course, is the author of the masterful study of Beethoven's Op. 109 sonata entitled *The Compositional Matrix*, Monographs in Theory and Composition 1 (Baldwin, N.Y.: Music Teachers National Association, 1961; rpt. New York: Da Capo, 1974).

Kerman concedes the success of the fourth point of Forte's agenda, as shall we. He then fails Forte's agenda on its final point: (5) the application of the analysis to twentieth-century music. Given Schenker's distrust of all music which he would consider modern, any critique of this proposal would seem on sure ground. To be accurate in reporting Forte's proposal, though, we need note that he carefully hedges his point, raising up for consideration only the application of Schenker's method to certain problematic modern works. As we well know, Forte situates these works at the boundary between two different systems of pitch organization — between "tonality" and "atonality." This distinction is such a commonplace as almost to seem beyond remark, yet it should not stand beyond question. Indeed, in coming to grips with this assumption we gain some sense of what binds together the successive failures of Forte's agenda. Kerman's association of neo-Schenkerian rhythmic theory and post-war compositional experiments takes us some length in this regard. Forte, at least implicitly, arrays three commensurable theories in a temporal sequence. On the one hand, he sets two theories (Schenker's theory and some post-tonal theory) in symmetry. When he talks of theorizing sketch studies, he is effectively capturing Schenker for this other mode of theorizing. He draws (however implicitly) some sort of equivalence between eighteenth- or early nineteenth-century and twentieth-century compositional process (where frequently the reconstruction of the composer's moves is not only possible but uniquely felicitous), at one and the same time opening the former to a type of examination peculiar to the latter, and validating the latter through the comparison with the former. On the other hand, when speaking of recovering the origins of tonality Forte posits yet a second symmetry between Schenker's model and some theory anterior to tonality.

It is in this notion of the reconciliation of different theories that we arrive at our own diagnosis for the "failures" of Forte's agenda. Forte wrongly assumes a compatibility between Schenker's *a posteriori* theory and an *a priori* theory (or the assumptions of an *a priori* theory). In part, he forces Schenker to do the work of an *a priori* theory. As noted, Schenker's construction justifies itself as an accurate account of both a psychological and a musical experience, and moreover, it is a synthesis predicated on the assignment of a unique transcendental presence to the canon. It is an *objective* synthesis. Forte does not recognize this synthesis, only the analysis to which it gives birth. He does not recognize its enclosure in the canon, but places it outside of the canon. Hence, he sees in Schenker a theory that justifies itself by its internal coherence (in the same way in which a serial theory or even Forte's own later twelve-pitch-class set theory would justify itself), and a theory which, grounded in an analysis that stands before the phenomenal appearance of music either in its historical or psychological manifestations or in its concrete texts, can constitute itself as an autonomous evaluation to be applied with equal validity (though perhaps not with equal results) to the entire field of musical evidence, be it early music, post-canonic music, or compositional process.

At the same time we might venture that Forte's theoretical commensurability works the other way, that he wishes to appropriate for any potential *a priori* theory the analytical richness of Schenker's synthesis. Let us take the notion of an inversional symmetry between *a priori* and *a posteriori* theories to begin with. Earlier we spoke of the *a priori* theory as compositional. This assertion has a common-sense truth. A theory of harmonic function will obviously lend itself to compositional extension, to the creation of new harmonies validated by their retention of function. A theory of ordered aggregates, or of the relations between ordered aggregates, even more obviously lends itself to composition. Such a theory may lend itself to understanding musical texts. Particularly in the case of theories that discover some higher-level abstract relation within the field of pitch organization, their analytic application will often turn on the identification of compositional intention. If we understand the mechanics of, let us say, combinatoriality as an abstract relation of set forms, and if we discover combinatorial set forms in, let us say, the music of Schoenberg, we are essentially recreating a compositional process. In fact, the most charged insights of such a theory are often synthetic, as, for example, when it was realized that a theory of tonality could be derived from the unique multiplicity of interval classes within the diatonic pitch field and, hence, that this analysis precedes the psychology of harmony or consonance as well as the history of tonality.[29] Accordingly, we might argue the thesis that

29 The unique multiplicity of interval classes in the diatonic collection is first pointed out by Milton Babbitt ("The Structure and Function of Music Theory," 15). It is this sort of synthetic insight which Forte hopes to substantiate in his exhaustive analysis of the twelve-pitch-class field in *The Structure of Atonal Music* (New Haven and London: Yale University Press, 1973): He unearths a whole series of relationships in this field ("K" and "Kh" complexes, "Z-relations") which in potential should be manifested (unconsciously) in the atonal works of the twentieth-century masters. We should also not overlook the fact that a "theory" need not govern an aggregate of pieces or even govern an entire piece, but can venture such a synthetic insight about a passage (as in Boretz's reading of *Tristan*). Perhaps the most far-reaching claim of this sort is found in the eighteenth-

where the *a posteriori* theory can give birth to a powerful analytic practice, the *a priori* theory can likewise give birth to a powerful, if local, synthesis. This may well be the reason for Forte's misreading of Schenker. We might argue that Forte, in his desire to validate the discipline of theory institutionally, conceives the synthetic claims Schenker makes on the history and experience of music as a product of an analytic theory, rather than conceiving the analysis as a product of a synthetic theory.

Regardless of the particular arguments, we can assert that the problems undercutting the realization of Forte's agenda result from an epistemological misdiagnosis of Schenker's program. Kerman, by contrast, comes closer to the mark. Indeed, in collapsing Schenker's theory together with several weak sisters under the rubric of "formalist analysis" and in conceiving of this discourse as an intrusion into his favored domain of "traditionalist criticism," he locates it decisively within the field of the *a posteriori*. Then, in keeping with his broad agenda, he lays out three points upon which Schenker's analysis (and indeed formalist analysis as a whole) fails. First, it makes no provision for genre (and is thus confined to reading only pieces or passages of pieces). Second, it makes no provision for the extra-notational components in music, ignoring the texts of vocal music in particular. Third, it presumes an "organic unity" and thus for every musical passage or piece posits a single reading.

Kerman's first assertion is correct. When Schenker speaks of the process of fugue or sonata, he argues not their uniqueness as genres or forms but instead their derivation from a common musical sensibility. Kerman, though, does not question why Schenker neglects these notions. In Kerman's criticism (as in much of musical historiography) the idea of genre takes on a transcendental value. "Genre" thus stands as a second-order synthetic move, fusing both an embodied process (or form) and a historical development, yet brought into being as a classificatory agent functioning within a comparative study of collections of musical works. For the sake of argument we might conceive a project in which one attempts to substantiate the definitions of particular genres through some comparative application of Schenker's analysis. (After all, we have at least tacitly assumed some comparative underpinnings in Schenker's analysis, and we might

century mathematician Leonhard Euler's *Tentamen novae theoriae musicae ex certissimis harmoniae principiis dilucide expositae* (St. Petersburg, 1739; rpt. New York: Broude, 1968) wherein he claims to rediscover ancient Hellenic scale structures through a rather intriguing acoustic calculus involving successive divisions of the octave.

look to his article on fugue as establishing a precedent.) But such a project would tell us little. Schenker conceives of his canon as a bounded whole, a concrete thing that comes to visibility at a single, specific psychological and temporal moment. To introduce some notion of genre would be to subdivide this single event, would be (in effect) to analyze his analysis. It would conflate two different transcendental constructions. Thus, Schenker stands on firm epistemological ground in denying such a second-order synthesis a status within his primary synthesis.

Kerman secondly finds Schenker's analysis wanting in its treatment of the genre of vocal music, insensitive to the delicate relation of text and music, and from these inadequacies develops a critique of Schenker's exclusive concentration on the function of pitch configurations. This point turns on the question of representation. To open Schenker's analysis to questions about the relation between text and music would be to reopen or re-problematize representation, thus to compromise that move which enables Schenker to rewrite the domain of criticism in the first place.

Kerman's third point merits the closest examination. He argues that Schenker's various disabilities derive from the automatic assumption of an "organic unity" subsuming all moments of the musical text and all readings in one grand motion. Both of Kerman's previous objections stem from this critique. His traditionalist criticism argues the musical text as a constellation of moments or localities, the musical interpretation likewise. The notion of an open critical field is attractive in itself, yet there are deeper issues to be addressed here. Kerman's objection to the ideological "organic unity" is an objection to the epistemology of Schenker's closed synthesis, his argument for a fluid and musical reading of the musical text as an argument for a constellation of contingent syntheses such as "genre" or "style" or "voice" or "process" or "intention." We might venture that within a traditional critical practice these terms are taken as primary syntheses, and that Kerman senses, in Schenker, an implausible "zero-level" synthesis.

Kerman's critique, however, may be vulnerable on these same grounds. He seems to resist a theorization of his own criticism, seems most comfortable with the availability of a wide range of synthetic tools that can be used as needed, yet that can also be trusted not to compromise the argumentative flexibility of the critic. As we well know, however, other critics would theorize their projects in terms of notions such as gender or political analysis or the like, constructions which, in order to be effective rather than simply polemic, need to impose a certain rigor on criticism –

constructions we might loosely think of as second-order syntheses, subsuming, as they do, first-order syntheses such as "style" or "voice".[30]

Thus, to appropriate Kerman's position vis à vis Forte for ourselves, we might assign a low grade to the extension of Kerman's agenda for a traditionalist criticism subsequent to the publication of his polemic. Unlike the substantive failure of Forte's agenda, the failure of Kerman's agenda is one of constraint. To wit, where theorists subsequent to Forte seemingly fail to arrive at a Schenkerian theory of rhythm, or a new examination of tonality, or a convincing explication of composer's sketches, or a fresh reading of problematic modern music, the significant constituency of critics subsequent to Kerman refuse in large part to be bound within the limits he sets for the critical discourse, theorizing their criticism, and ultimately suggesting a new and subversive historiography for music. Where Forte errs in assuming a functional and temporal commensurability of music theories, Kerman errs in not seeing beyond a theoretic commensurability of interpretations.

In other words, if we are to suggest that Forte misreads Schenker, then we suggest that Kerman does likewise. The former reads Schenker with an inappropriate optimism, the latter with an inappropriate pessimism. The former reads Schenker in terms of discursive possibilities, the latter in terms of discursive threats. To return to an earlier notion, Forte, while working from the notion of an elaboration of theory and the world of potential theories, cannot but see a Schenker who is open to elaboration, whereas Kerman, intent on establishing his own discourse within a world of impoverished positivisms, cannot but see a Schenker who reduces musical reality.

As was the case with Schenker's analytic practice, however, elaboration and reduction are not the only plausible interpretations of Schenker's theory vis à vis music and the musical discourse. We would not read the given surface of the musical text as an elaboration of the *Ursatz*, or the *Ursatz* as a reduction of that musical surface. For Schenker, the masterwork is at once a condensation of a complex of psychological dynamics and of a lengthy evolution of musical forces. Reading Schenker outside of Forte's

---

30 I think here of the sorts of theorized criticism which have only recently come to be seen as the "new musicology," including, in this category, the names of such interesting scholars as Susan McClary, Rose Subotnik, Gary Tomlinson, and Carolyn Abbate. As noted before, this school of criticism (if we would call it that) might better be thought of as a "new historicism." Prof. Kerman is in many respects the godfather of this school, particularly in respect to its concentration on nineteenth-century music.

or Kerman's agenda (or of any agenda), we understand his synthesis as a condensation of a complex network of arguments and epistemologies which itself is an artifact of a particular historical and theoretical moment. Thus there is something forced or false in presuming Schenker's theory either as something to be elaborated into a super-theory or as something which reduces a rich surface of musical discourses. We can but attempt to explicate the context and arguments from which it has condensed.

To think of Schenker's synthesis as an epistemological condensation is not, however, to deny its status as a musical insight or to deny it a place as an agent within our discourse (any more than his reading of the canon as a condensation would deny it status as part of a continuing musical culture). Foucault's discursive model still holds, and the structure of the epistemo-logical universe that gives birth to Schenker has not altered (even if its concrete particulars have). The sudden appearance of new musical empiricisms of the later nineteenth century still ripples throughout the musical discourse as a recurring crisis. The constitution of those historiographic and psychological investigations of music that confine themselves to the purely empirical examination of musical phenomena will always bring into question those portions of the musical discourse that lie outside such empiricisms. For Forte (and, indeed, for the theoretical community in which he is a leading member), this crisis is symptomized by an exhausted and imprecise theoretical vocabulary, and in response he moves his theory (and that of Schenker) toward a degree of epistemologi-cal justification through which it can hold its own against the scientific disciplines. For Kerman, this crisis is symptomatized by a narrow and impotent methodology, and in response he argues a discourse that does not attempt to set itself up as a counter-science but rather subordinates these sciences. Although Schenker's rhetoric is one of crisis, his rejection of all of his immediate predecessors, his declared affiliation with remote ances-tors and his disengagement from the musical world beyond theory, in combination all seem components of a strategy he would use to distance himself from such matters (or of conceiving this crisis in ideological rather than epistemological terms). Yet while maintaining a superficial detach-ment from the musical sciences, Schenker quietly subsumes their respective cores, and thus locates a private yet secure solution to this problem. To think of Schenker's synthesis as an epistemological condensation is not to deny it a place in our own discourse. Quite the contrary, it is to grant it status as a different sort of agent, one which is able through a series of closures — a closure of psychological explanation, a closure of musical historiography, a closure of the canon and a closure of representation – to address this same crisis implicitly (through its structure) not explicitly.

THE FUNCTION OF IDEOLOGY

The idea that Schenker successfully addresses fundamental epistemological issues by addressing the structure of these issues, however, prompts a number of questions. The most important of these concern abstraction and method. The particularity of Schenker's theory as an artifact rules out both its extension in Forte's program and (although necessarily less strongly) its displacement by a loose critical practice in Kerman's program. Is there some way, though, of abstracting Schenker's argument (rather than, as is the case in Forte, his analysis) and using the notion of an *a posteriori* closed synthesis as a model for a collection of closed syntheses (thus satisfying, to an extent, Kerman's objection to the exclusiveness of Schenker's theory)?

Several intimations of other closed syntheses surfaced in our reading of the various points in Forte's agenda. Other possibilities suggest themselves. We might imagine a theory of music which in reference to a "canon" of later fourteenth-century secular polyphony accommodates (or synthesizes) a psychology or rhetoric of rhythmic affect and a history derived from the changing rules of mensural notation (in particular the movement from modal notation to Franconian and *ars nova* notation), thus locating the essence of this canon as a sort of macro-rhythm of phrase-weighting. (Such an analysis might frame itself as an alternative to the standard reading of cadential structure and fixed forms, and in giving priority to temporal rather than pitch events would treat the long rhythmic displacements and multiple shifts of tactus as structural rather than ornamental features.) We might imagine an analysis of early seventeenth-century music born of a conjunction of a theory of perceptual grouping and a reading of late-Renaissance procedures of clef, range, and signature. We might even more plausibly imagine a reading of eighteenth-century instrumental music drawn from the superimposition of a stemmatic (or genealogical) analysis of the rhetorical structure and recurrence of themes over a period of time and a narratological theory of reception.

How realistic, though, is the notion of such a collection of *a posteriori* syntheses? A fourth such synthesis suggests itself. Forte proposes the application of Schenker's analysis to a group of problematic modern works (in particular those of Stravinsky and the pre-serial Schoenberg), positing that the composers of these works remember (if only to a degree, and if only subconsciously) the prolongational techniques of their predecessors. The flaw in this argument is its presumption of two commensurable systems (a "tonal" system and an "atonal" system) between which are caught these problematic works. One might attempt to remedy this flaw by constructing a post-Schenkerian closed synthesis (a theory of "modernist" music) that would be commensurable to that of Schenker. The mechanics of such a synthesis, however, are open to question. A first difficulty is easily over-come. Schenker's canon is not defined along any easy stylistic lines: works that predate Bach are grouped with superficially quite different works of Brahms. A commensurable canon, to enjoy the same authority, would likewise have to transcend immediate stylistic and temporal distinctions. This in itself is not an impossible task. (Forte, for example, seems to presuppose at the time of his agenda a canon that includes "pre-serial" and "serial" works: one might conceive of adding to this sequence "post-serial" works.) In all likelihood, this modernist canon would overlap with that of Schenker, including those figures (Liszt, Wagner, Strauss) whom he rejects, and extend through our own "post-modernists." A second difficulty, though, is more substantive. A modernist synthesis, like that of Schenker, would join loosely historiographic and psychological analyses of its canon. Yet the works of this canon are themselves already aware of their historical place and psychological content. Indeed, this selfconsciousness may be what binds such a canon together. Wagner conceives his music as a sort of symbolist realization of the cultural (or racial) and psychological uncon-scious; Stravinsky is by turns anthropological and historicist; Schoenberg centers his music at the crucial moment in a self-conceived music-historical evolution; Morton Feldman loses himself in an exploration of listening and memory; John Adams ironically exploits the history of the historiography and theory of music. All, in other words, conceive their music within the modern epistemological system. Mahler's music may be that of the *a posteriori*, the music of a place where cultural and personal experience join as one; Babbitt's that of the *a priori*, the place where the structure of the twelve-pitch-class system is made audible. (These asser-tions are misleading: both Mahler and Babbitt think within the epistemo-logical system as a whole, and while their respective musics may seem to have an affinity with some particular domain of this system, they are not thus confined. Composition is not available to epistemological evaluation, but it does suggest how the composer thinks of music.)

Schenker himself senses this. When he speaks of the collapse of diminutional composition, he speaks not only of a general exhaustion of the musical imagination or of a temporal phenomenon but of the displacement of the true diminutional composer by the "idea" composer. He speaks of the displacement of a natural or unaware composition by one that is artificial and selfconscious. Yet are the composers of Schenker's canon to be denied their own particular epistemological awareness? Can one assert that Philipp Emanuel Bach and Mozart do not write within a universe that conceives music in terms of such notions as harmony's representation of the truth of whole-number acoustics, a taxonomy of affect, the definition of beauty in the commensurability of events, and the origins of music in the human capacities of sensation and association? Schenker's attribution of a natural genius to the composers of his canon rests not on their insensibility to the musical discourse of their world (with its own epistemological foundations), but on their unawareness of the epistemological foundations of his own particular (and quite different) world. Thus, it may be that a conception of "modernist" music equivalent in explanatory power to that of Schenker will only become possible when some future theorist stands likewise in a different epistemological universe than that of the music engaged. Thus also, however, there can never be a theory of such music that is epistemologically commensurable to that of Schenker.

This does not, of course, in itself rule out the closed synthesis as applied to historically remote Renaissance and Medieval musics. Schenker's own analytic drama, though, awards an importance to proximity. The composers of his canon are close enough in time that he can imagine them in his own world but leave them unconscious of this world. A similar analysis might only be available if one were to imagine (let us say) the Renaissance composer as an inhabitant of a seventeenth-century epistemological world, yet unaware of that world. (Our earlier proposals implied such a strategy.) It is questionable, though, whether the modern theorist can enter this same world and construct an analysis of any power and conviction.

Neither does it rule out a different explanatory synthesis applying to Schenker's canon. But the picture of the unaware composer and the aware theorist suggests other complications. The distance between Schenker and the master-composer is temporal (although Schenker's claim to some tenuous validation on the part of Brahms is a nice touch). It is also, however, by nature epistemological. This is the dramatic problem underlying Schenker's theory. The great nineteenth-century sciences of music unfold within the temporal span of this distance, yet as they themselves define this distance, and hence deny that the composers of Schenker's canon and

Schenker himself occupy the same world, they cannot be acknowledged. Inasmuch as the success of Schenker's closed synthesis, his analytic drama, depends on concealing the epistemological disjunction that separates him from the composers of his canon, he must present this estrangement differently, present it ideologically.

This is a point which needs to be handled delicately. Schenker all too readily brings to his work a particular social and political consciousness. While neither Forte nor Kerman remark Schenker's ideology (although in the case of the latter, we might see his focus on the notion of organic unity as making an ideological point), both read Schenker against the backdrop of a sort of liberal humanism. This study itself has moved on the premise of bracketing out Schenker's ideology. It would have been almost too simple to explain the closure of Schenker's post-war canon – his erasure of Wagner and the entire school of German modernism and his situation of his work as a postscript to the history of music – as the product of a political agenda, too easy to explicate it by pointing out that he ties this musical modernism to the corruptions of social democracy (and perhaps that of National Socialism, which we cannot forget embodied its own modernist and populist agenda). It is only in disregarding this explanation that the closure of the canon is seen as an epistemological move, a necessary preliminary to his dissolution of the problem of representation, and as a means of opening a space for his objective synthesis.

In fact, we have on occasion invoked Schenker's ideology as a consequence of his epistemology rather than the reverse. The entire rhetoric of German cultural essentialism, of political authoritarianism, and of betrayal is much too obvious to serve as more than a foil. (This is not to rule out any potential study of Schenker's ideology. Such a study, undertaken with a certain sensitivity, would have many rewards. One can imagine placing Schenker's polemic within a constellation of similar polemics attributable to such figures as Riemann and Pfitzner, or situating it within an institutional politics that demands some sort of rhetorical escalation, or reading it as a defensive compensation for a problematic Jewish identity. One might alternatively look to derive Schenker's ideology from some political projection of the Brahms–Wagner dichotomy onto an axis of traditionalist and radical conservatism. With regard to this last point, Brahms seems to occupy a strange and important position psychologically within Schenker's universe, and it would be interesting to engage his reluctance to write about any of Brahms's larger works both psychologically and ideologically.)

Given the notion that ideology serves a function in explaining the estrangement of Schenker from the composers of his canon, however, it would appear that the relation between ideology and epistemology is more complex than any simple causal sequence. We might first be tempted to assert that Schenker himself distinguishes his ideology from his epistemology (such as it is), that the former bears the same relation to musical composition as the latter does to the musical discourse (both being radical critiques or suggested corrections), and that these two ways of looking at the world coincide in their respective notions of synthesis. In other words, perhaps when Schenker speaks of the decline of German (and Austrian) society and culture and of the need for a return to a healthier and more authoritarian political and musical order he is addressing Schoenberg and Pfitzner and Hindemith and the performing establishment, and when he speaks of the means for uncovering the musical laws that govern the work of the masters (such items as the fidelity to the text) he is addressing the mandarins of the German musical academy. On reflection, however, this distribution of functions cannot be correct. Schenker may see himself as most directly addressing the compositional and performing establishments (in the guise of a prophet of the Torah addressing the corruptors of the Temple), yet we should be suspicious of his dramatics. All rhetoric aside, Schenker does not truly engage the composer, and in fact goes to lengths to deflect any prescriptive reading of his theory. He denies the composer (in the same way, speaking biographically, as he has denied his own capacity for composition). Nor does he address the musical performer at length (although he prizes the validation of prominent performers). The principal object of his writings and of his polemics, in the end, cannot but be the great figures of the musical discourse.

It follows that when Schenker decries a lost capacity for synthesis in contemporary culture and contemporary music, he is decrying its loss most specifically in the ways in which people speak about music. (Although the appeal to "real musicians" is a time-honored strategy among those who write about music, it is a strategy aimed at an audience of others who write about music.) The notion of the canon thus comes to serve another function. The various empirical sciences of music of the later nineteenth century come into existence as investigations of this canon. They investigate its depths (for example in the psychoacoustic study of the basis of consonance), restore its surfaces (in the reconstruction of the original text and in the comprehensive restorations of the great critical editions), substantiate its progenitors (in musical biography), give it a history (in the analysis of style), and codify its practices (in music theory). Yet the elaboration of a sophisticated collection of methodologies opens the canon, adding new composers, new works, even new musics: systematic musicology and the study of musical psychology together create an anthropology of music, one in which there is no hierarchy, and indeed, no canon. The boundary between canonic and non-canonic work is gradually effaced and eventually erased. This is a point that Schenker does not let go unremarked: witness his condemnations of the revival of church modes, the notion of exotic harmony, the reification of folksong, the false mediation of the performing edition. Most importantly, however, he conceives this erasure of boundaries not as a consequence of a methodological empiricism but as an ideological act, an act of bad faith. Therefore, unlike the capacity for synthesis lost by composition, the loss of the same capacity within the musical discourse is remediable if this act of bad faith is rectified, if the musical discourse abandons that part of itself which would undermine the canon.

In light of this desire for an ideological correction, we can read Schenker's epistemological development a bit differently. The issue becomes one of rectification and compensation. Constructing (in a fashion) a descriptive psychology and appropriating (again in a fashion) the suppositions of musical paleography and the form of the stemmatic analysis, Schenker asserts control over just those portions of the sciences of music which carry the most authority. Having lost their anchors, the constellation of investigations which surround these points (biographical studies, comparative musicology, stylistics, psychoacoustics) are neutralized. In so far as these methodologies (paleography, stemmatic history, descriptive psychology) are themselves guilty of bad faith in relation to the canon, they by compensation are gradually erased in the evolution of Schenker's project and subsumed completely in the closed synthesis. This is why Hauptmann, Marx, Sechter, Riemann, Richter, Capellen, Helmholtz, and all of Schenker's early interlocutors vanish by the time of *Free Composition*, why he presents his theory as a method for developing the ear rather than as a psychology of music, why he frames his history in terms of narratives rather than methodologies.

It is also why he can affiliate his project openly only with eighteenth-century theory. But this filiation is itself misleading. His theory does not map onto or recapitulate or somehow culminate eighteenth-century theory. Schenker draws this distinction carefully, and does not comfortably assume that the lost plenitude of the masterworks (both musical and social) can be recovered through a naive return to the past. He may state that Fux or C.P.E.Bach are on the right track, yet he will always point out the respect in which their theories are inadequate. An understanding of Fux or of the mechanics of thoroughbass is not an understanding of Mozart or Beethoven. Rather, he situates his theory just contiguous to eighteenth-century theory. He arrives at an abstraction (or even a representation) of the modern discourse of music that synthesizes its own historiography, psychology, criticism, and theory and that demonstrates its good faith by denying its own history and moving into an immediate proximity to the masterworks. Thus the dialogue of music is schematized, abstracted in terms of the eighteenth-century masters (Bach and Fux), the eighteenth-century villain (Rameau), and the single post-classical master (Schenker).

This ideological drama completes Schenker's synthesis. He creates a musical world that is a representation of the world of the modern discourse yet is theoretically distinguished from that world. This has certain consequences. Schenker can preempt the authority of the sciences while protesting that his theory (when put into practice) is artistic rather than scientific. Indeed, his analysis offers a convincing simulation of the empiricism offered by the sciences of music, a sense of a music defamiliarized. Yet where the paleographer or textual critic offers us the evidence of a music that is in some manner alien, where the experimental psychologist presents us with an analysis of the perception and reception of music that demonstrates how these complex phenomena are experientially unavailable, Schenker defamiliarizes the masterwork by displacing the experiencing subject rather than the musical object. As noted, he located his synthesis within the domain of the transcendental *a posteriori* rather than that of the transcendental *a priori*, but at the same time he offers something that in many respects looks like a conventional theory of music in its abstraction and definition of the experiencing subject (although he theoretically constructs rather than analyzes this subject), thus distinguishing his project from that of the critic (whose experiencing subject remains undefined).

Also, in constructing his theory as a displaced representation of the modern discourse, Schenker precludes any substantive exchange between his theory and the investigations of his contemporaries. There cannot truly be a Schenkerian historiography or criticism or psychology: there can only be repetitions of the historiography, criticism, and psychology already a part of the theory.

Nor, though, can a post-Schenkerian theory be conceivable within this world (or at least a theory that stands in the same proximity to Schenker as he does to the eighteenth-century theorist, and can thus set itself up as a successor). Where Riemann, let us say, conceives his harmonic theory within a succession of harmonic theories extending back to the earliest polyphonic treatises (and hence vests a certain importance in the history of theory), and if pressed would admit to the plausibility of some future refinement of his harmony, Schenker's ideological move forecloses this possibility. He does not leave any purchase within his argument for a successor to use to argue itself as a correction or rectification. The science which he appropriates (the descriptive psychology and explanatory historiography), unlike that to which Riemann appeals (the psychoacoustic explanation of consonance), is not subject to empirical revision, nor can his synthesis be ideologically accused of straying from its purpose. Almost trivially, this substantiates our reservations about the notion of a collection of post-Schenkerian closed syntheses. In a way, the project is too complex. If we were to use his epistemological transactions with the psychological and historical sciences of music as a model, we would have to construct from a corresponding series of transactions an abstract representation of our own discursive world particular to each such closed synthesis, one which can efface its own history and be situated in proximity to that "canon" which is its subject. Following the reasoning above, however, it would seem that we would have to generalize his ideology into a system of ideologies, extrapolate the act of bad faith demonstrated by the modern sciences of music in relation to the canon as a series of acts of bad faith in relation to a series of arbitrarily chosen canons. This notion, of course, is ridiculous, yet it gives us a sense that even so remote a representation of Schenker encounters problems. The closer we come to arriving at a substantive analysis of his project, the more strongly he resists our attempts to make use of this analysis.

We can look at this from another perspective. Any representation we would make of Schenker's theory stands, in effect, as a double move, a representation of Schenker's own representation of the discursive universe. Hence there is the temptation to characterize (at least implicitly) Schenker's theory as a generative grammar or as a phenomenology: both of these characterizations re-represent the claims that Schenker masks by displacing his epistemology from its historical context. The problem with this move is that these characterizations cannot reconstitute Schenker's argument accurately. This is likewise the problem with Forte's reading. He more subtly represents Schenker's theory as a construct that situates itself anterior to psychology and historiography and thus analyzes these domains, yet the inaccuracies of this representation (in particular its failure to acknowledge the closures inherent to the theory) become clear when Schenker resists the tasks to which he is assigned.

In other words, in forcing us quietly to posit any interpretive appropriation of his theory as a doubled representation Schenker frustrates any sort of move we would make to normalize him to our own discourse of music theory or criticism. Thus it would seem that our reading of an epistemologically rich yet ideologically displaced Schenker is at least mildly pessimistic. This is not, however, truly the case. Kerman's manifesto proposes the ultimate normalization of Schenker, the consignment of his analysis to history as a failed critical paradigm. His reading of Schenker is almost ideological. He protests against what he sees as an artificial constraint of interpretive horizons, and makes the case that this should disqualify Schenker as a point on which to center our own critical and analytic practice. One must question, though, the characterization of Schenker's analysis as a paradigm, or as a means of centering our discourse. The notion of a paradigm, the notion that an explication comes into being to answer certain questions and thus centers a discourse, but is displaced as the interpretive horizon shifts and new questions come to the fore, is attractive. Whether it can or cannot be substantiated in the discourse of music is something we might question. Yet Schenker himself would protest this reading. He does not wish his analysis to be taken as another in an evolving sequence of theories and analyses and criticisms (even as so powerful a member as to function as a paradigm), does not wish to admit an open history of theory. (One cannot imagine, let us say, a historical series of Schenkerian readings of a single passage which shows some sort of evolution. One can imagine harmonic analyses which do reveal an evolution.) His theory does not displace an earlier paradigm such as harmony but ideologically erases that paradigm (as an act of good faith). The strength of his reading rests in its series of closures, in the fact that while it addresses the central issues or questions of its contemporary discourse it then proceeds to deny the validity of these issues and questions.

Schenker attempts to preempt any historical normalization of his theory within the discourse at large by himself first normalizing (and thus dominating) that discourse. In this he has been remarkably successful: a good portion of the theoretical and critical community remains suspended within the Schenkerian moment. Inasmuch as this moment offers a rich and replete access to musical intuitions, this suspension is not in itself a bad thing. Schenker's theoretical project, though, can teach us more than simply an analytical method. The richness of his analysis is matched by (and is a product of) an epistemological richness, a willingness to venture an involved and often radical argument. He engages the musical discourse in its entirety, and situates his way of speaking about music at a place within that discourse which is both unexpected and powerful. If we are willing to learn, Schenker's project would teach us, in the broadest sense of the term, to be theorists.

BIBLIOGRAPHY

Abraham, Otto, and Karl Schaefer. "Ueber die maximale Geschwindigkeit von Tonfolgen." *Beiträge zur Akustik und Musikwissenschaft*. Vol. III. (1901), 13–21.

Adler, Guido. "Umfang, Methode und Ziel der Musikwissenschaft." *Vierteljahrsschrift für Musikwissenschaft* 1. Leipzig, Breitkopf und Härtel, 1885; rpt. Hildesheim: Georg Olms, 1966. 5–20.

Der Stil in der Musik. Book 1: *Prinzipien und Arten des musikalischen Stils*. Leipzig: Breitkopf und Härtel, 1911.

Methode der Musikgeschichte. Leipzig: Breitkopf und Härtel, 1919.

"Style-Criticism." Trans. Oliver Strunk. *Musical Quarterly* 20 (1934), 172–176.

Adorno, Theodor. *Introduction to the Sociology of Music*. Trans. E. B. Ashton. New York: Seabury Press, 1976.

Allen, Warren Dwight. *Philosophies of Music History*. New York: American Book Co., 1939; 2nd edn. New York: Dover, 1962.

Arend, Max. "Ist der Kreis der Konsonanzen nur historisch oder a priori geschlossen?" *Neue Zeitschrift für Musik* 83 (1916), 165–167.

Babbitt, Milton. "The Structure and Function of Music Theory." *Perspectives on Contemporary Music Theory*. Ed. Benjamin Boretz and Edward T. Cone. New York: Norton, 1972. 10–21.

Bach, Carl Philipp Emanuel. *Sechs ausgewählte Sonaten für Klavier allein*. Ed. Hans von Bülow. Leipzig: C. F. Peters, 1862.

Clavier-Sonaten, Rondos und freie Fantasien für Kenner und Liebhaber. Ed. E. F. Baumgart. Breslau: F. E. C. Leuckart, 1863.

Klavierwerke. Ed. Heinrich Schenker. Vienna: Universal Edition, 1902.

Bach, Johann Sebastian. *Das wohltemperirte Klavier* I. Ed. Robert Franz and Otto Dressel. Leipzig: Breitkopf und Härtel, 1890.

The Well-Tempered Clavichord, Vol. 1. Ed. C. Czerny. Boston: Schirmer, 1893.

Das wohltemperierte Klavier I. Ed. Béla Bartók. Budapest: Zenemükiadó Vállalat, 1967.

Das wohltemperierte Klavier I. Ed. Ferruccio Busoni. Wiesbaden: Breitkopf und Härtel, n.d.

Die Fugen des wohltemperierten Klaviers: partiturmässig dargestellt und nach ihrem Bau erläutert I. Ed. F. Stade. Leipzig: Steingräber-Verlag, n.d.

Bartók, Béla. *The Hungarian Folksong.* Ed. Benjamin Suchoff, trans. M. D. Calvocoressi. Albany: State University of New York, 1981.

Becking, Gustav. " 'Hören' und 'Analysieren': Zu Hugo Riemanns Analyse von Beethovens Klaviersonaten." *Zeitschrift für Musikwissenschaft* 1 (1919), 587–603.

Bekker, Paul. "Was ist Phänomenologie der Musik?" *Die Musik* 17/4 (January, 1924), 241–249.

Bergeron, Katherine. Representation, Reproduction, and the Revival of Gregorian Chant at Solesmes. Ph.D. dissertation, Cornell University, 1989.

Beyschlag, Adolph. *Die Ornamentik der Musik.* Leipzig: Breitkopf und Härtel, 1908.

Blankenburg, Christian Friedrich. *Litterarische Zusätze zu Johann Georg Sulzers Allgemeine Theorie der schönen Künste,* vol. II. Leipzig: Weidmann, 1797; rpt. Frankfurt am Main: Athenium, 1972.

Böckh, August. *Encyklopädie und Methodologie der philologischen Wissenschaften.* Ed. Ernst Bratuscheck. Leipzig: B. G. Teubner, 1877.

Bopp, Franz. *Vergleichende Grammatik des Sanskrit, Zend, Armenischen, Griechischen, Lateinischen, Litthauischen, Altslawischen, Gothischen und Deutschen.* 3rd edn. Berlin: F. Dummler, 1868–1871.

Boretz, Benjamin. "Meta-variations: Studies in the Foundations of Musical Thought, Part I: Thought (1)." *Perspectives of New Music* 8/1 (Fall–Winter 1969), 1–74. "Part II: Sketch of a Musical System." *Perspectives of New Music* 8/2 (Spring–Summer 1970), 23–48. "Meta-variations, Part III: The Construction of a Musical Syntax (I)." *Perspectives of New Music* 9/1 (Fall–Winter 1970), 23–42. "Musical Syntax (II)." *Perspectives of New Music* 9/2–10/1 (Spring–Summer–Fall–Winter 1971), 232–270. "Meta-variations Part IV: Analytic Fallout (I)." *Perspectives of New Music* 11/1 (Fall–Winter 1972), 146–223. "Analytic Fallout (II)." *Perspectives of New Music* 11/2 (Spring–Summer 1973), 156–203.
"Language, as a Music". *Perspectives of New Music* 17/2 (Spring–Summer 1979), 131–196.

Boretz, Benjamin, and Edward Cone ed. *Perspectives on Contemporary Music Theory.* New York: Norton, 1972.

Browne, Richmond. "The Inception of the Society for Music Theory." *Music Theory Spectrum,* 1 (1979), 2–5.

Bücher, Karl. *Arbeit und Rhythmus.* Leipzig: Teubner, 1899.

Cage, John. "Sculpture Musicale." *Perspectives of New Music* 26/1 (Winter, 1988), 12–25.

Capellen-Osnabrück, Georg. *Ist das System S. Sechter's ein geeigneter Ausgangspunkt für die theoretische Wagnerforschung?.* Leipzig: C. F. Kahnt, 1902.
Die "musikalische" Akustik als Grundlage der Harmonik und Melodik. Leipzig: C. F. Kahnt, 1903.

Die Freiheit oder Unfreiheit der Töne und Intervall, als Kriterium der Stimmführung. Leipzig: C. F. Kahnt, 1905

Die Zukunft der Musiktheorie (Dualismus oder "Monismus"?) und ihre Einwirkung auf die Praxis. Leipzig: C. F. Kahnt, 1905

Fortschrittliche Harmonie- und Melodielehre. Leipzig: C. F. Kahnt, 1908.

"Robert Mayerhofers Organische Harmonielehre und die moderne Theorie." *Die Musik* 9/6 (December, 1909), 346–357.

Carpé, Adolph. *Der Rhythmus: Sein Wesen in der Kunst und seine Bedeutung im musikalischen Vortrage.* Leipzig: Gebrüder Reinecke, n.d.

Grouping, Articulation, and Phrasing in Musical Interpretation. Leipzig: Bosworth, 1898

Chladni, Ernst *Entdeckung über die Theorie des Klangs.* Leipzig: Weidmanns Erben und Reich, 1787.

Collingwood, Robin George. *Speculum Mentis: or, The Map of Knowledge.* Oxford: Clarendon Press, 1924.

Coussemaker, C.-E.-H. *Scriptorum de musica medii aevi novam seriem.* Paris: Durand, 1864–1876.

Danziger, Kurt. *Constructing the Subject: Historical Origins of Psychological Research.* Cambridge Studies in the History of Psychology. Cambridge: Cambridge University Press, 1990.

Deutsch, Leonhard. *Individual-Psychologie im Musikunterricht und in der Musikerziehung: ein Beitrag zur Grundlegung musikalischer Gemeinkultur.* Leipzig: Steingräber, 1931.

Dilthey, Wilhelm. "Ideen über eine beschreibende und zergliedernde Psychologie." *Gesammelte Schriften,* V. Leipzig and Berlin: B. G. Teubner, 1957. 139–240. Trans. Richard M. Zaner as "Ideas Concerning a Descriptive and Analytic Psychology" in *Descriptive Psychology and Historical Understanding.* The Hague: Martinus Nijhoff, 1977. 23–120.

Dubiel, Joseph. "'When You are a Beethoven': Kinds of Rules in Schenker's 'Counterpoint.'" *Journal of Music Theory* 34 (1990), 291–340.

Eimert, Herbert. "Bekenntnis und Methode: Zur gegenwärtigen Lage der Musikwissenschaft". *Zeitschrift für Musikwissenschaft* 9 (1926), 95–109.

Euler, Leonhard. *Tentamen novae theoriae musicae ex certissimis harmoniae principiis dilucide expositae.* St. Petersburg, 1739; rpt. New York: Broude, 1968.

Forte, Allen. *The Compositional Matrix.* Monographs in Theory and Composition 1. Baldwin, N.Y.: Music Teachers National Association, 1961; rpt. New York: Da Capo Press, 1974.

The Structure of Atonal Music. New Haven and London: Yale University Press, 1973.

Forte, Allen, and Steven E. Gilbert. *Introduction to Schenkerian Analysis.* New York and London: W. W. Norton, 1982.

Foucault, Michel. *Les Mots et les choses*. Paris: Editions Gallimard, 1966. Trans. (unattributed).

The Order of Things. London: Tavistock, 1970; New York: Vintage, 1973.

Freud, Sigmund. *Introductory Lectures on Psychoanalysis*. Trans. James Strachey. New York: W. W. Norton, 1966.

Frey, Martin. "Musikalisch-kritische Untersuchungen". *Die Musik* 8/21 (August 1909), 171–181.

Fuchs, Carl. *Die Zukunft des musikalischen Vortrags und sein Ursprung. Studien im Sinne der Riemannischen Reform und zur Aufklärung des Unterschiedes zwischen antiker und musikalischer Rhythmik*. Danzig: A. W. Kafemann, 1884.

Ganassi, Sylvestro. *Opera intitulata Fontegara* (1535). Ed. and Ger. trans Hildemarie Peter. Berlin-Lichterfelde: Robert Lienau, 1956. Eng. trans. Dorothy Swainson: Berlin-Lichterfelde: Robert Lienau, 1959.

Gatz, Felix. *Musik-Ästhetik in ihren Hauptrichtungen. Ein Quellenbuch der deutschen Musik-Ästhetik von Kant und der Frühromantik bis zur Gegenwart*. Stuttgart: Ferdinand Enke, 1929.

Gerbert, Martin. *Scriptores ecclesiastici de musice sacre potissimum*. St. Blasien, 1784.

Griesbacher, P. *Kirchenmusikalische Stilistik und Formenlehre*. I. Historischer Teil. Regensburg: Albert Coppenrath, 1: 1912, 2: 1912, 3: 1913, 4: 1916.

Gurlitt, Wilibald. "Hugo Riemann und die Musikgeschichte: Zu seinem 70. Geburtstag am 18. Juli 1919: Erster Teil: Voraussetzungen." *Zeitschrift für Musikwissenschaft* 1 (1919), 571–587.

Haas, Robert. *Aufführungspraxis der Musik*. Wildpark-Potsdam: Akademische Verlagsgesellschaft Athenaion, 1931.

Handke, Robert. "Die Diatonik in ihrem Einfluss auf die thematische Gestaltung des Bachschen Fugenbaues." *Bach-Jahrbuch* 7 (1910), 1–32.

Hanslick, Eduard. *Vom Musikalisch-Schönen*. Leipzig: Rudolph Weigel, 1854.

Hegel, Georg Wilhelm Friedrich. *Aesthetics: Lectures on Fine Arts*, vol. II. Trans. T. M. Knox. Oxford: Clarendon Press, 1975.

Helmholtz, Herman. *Die Lehre von den Tonempfindungen, als physiologische Grundlage für die Theorie der Musik*. Brunswick: Friedrich Vieweg, 1862.

Hoffmann, Bernhard. *Kunst und Vogelgesang in ihren wechselseitigen Beziehungen vom naturwissenschaftlich-musikalischen Standpunkte beleuchtet*. Leipzig: Quelle & Meyer, 1908.

Hohn, Wilhelm. *Der Kontrapunkt Palestrinas und seiner Zeitgenossen: eine Kontrapunktlehre mit praktischen Aufgaben*. Sammlung "Kirchenmusik", vol. XVII. Regensburg: Pustet, 1918.

Huber, Kurt. *Der Ausdruck musikalischer Elementarmotive: eine experimental-psychologische Untersuchung*. Leipzig: J. A. Barth, 1923.

Husserl, Edmund. *Phänomenologische Psychologie. Vorlesungen Sommersemester 1925*. Trans. John Scanlon as *Phenomenal Psychology*. The Hague: Martinus Nijhoff, 1977.

Jacobsthal, Gustav. *Die Mensuralnotenschrift des 12. und 13. Jahrhunderts.* Berlin: J. Springer, 1871.

Kallenbach, Lotte. "Das musikalische Hören." *Die Musik* 17/4 (January, 1925), 271–278.

Karg-Elert, Sigfrid. *Das Grundlagen der Musiktheorie,* Part II: *Harmonielehre.* 2nd edn. Leipzig: Speka-Musikalienverlag, 1921.

Kerman, Joseph. *Contemplating Music.* Cambridge, Mass.: Harvard University Press, 1985.

Kodály, Zoltán. *Folk Music of Hungary.* Trans. R. Tempest and C. Jolly. New York: Praeger, 1971.

Kretzschmar, Hermann. "Allgemeines und Besonderes zur Affektenlehre I." *Jahrbuch der Musikbibliothek Peters für 1911* (1912), 63–77.

"Allgemeines und Besonderes zur Affektenlehre II." *Jahrbuch der Musikbibliothek Peters für 1912* (1913), 65–78.

Kullak, Franz. *Der Vortrag in der Musik am Ende des 19. Jahrhunderts.* Leipzig: F. E. C. Leuckart, 1898.

Kurth, Ernst. *Grundlagen des linearen Kontrapunkts. Einführung in Stil und Technik von Bach's melodischer Polyphonie.* Bern: Max Drechsel, 1917; Berlin, Max Hesse, 1922, 1927.

LaRue, Jan. *Guidelines for Style Analysis.* New York: W. W. Norton, 1970.

Lerdahl, Fred, and Ray Jackendoff. *A Generative Theory of Tonal Music.* Cambridge, Mass. and London: MIT Press, 1983.

Lipps, Theodor. *Psychological Studies.* Trans. Herbert Sanborn. Baltimore: Williams and Wilkins, 1926.

Lomax, Alan. *Folk Song Style and Culture.* Publication No. 88. Washington D.C.: American Association for the Advancement of Science, 1968.

Lorenz, Alfred. *Das Geheimnis der Form bei Richard Wagner. II. Der musikalische Aufbau von Richard Wagners "Tristan und Isolde."* Berlin: Max Hesse, 1926.

Abendländische Musikgeschichte im Rhythmus der Generationen: eine Anregung. Berlin: Hesse, 1928.

Ludwig, Friedrich. *Repertorium organorum recentioris et motetorum vetustissimi stili.* Part 1. Halle: Niemeyer, 1910.

Lussy, Mathis. *Traité de l'expression musicale; accents, nuances et mouvements dans la músique vocale et instrumentale.* Paris: Berger-Levrault and Heugel, 1874; 7th edn. Paris: Fischbacher, 1897.

Le Rhythme musical, son origine, sa fonction et son accentuation. Paris: Heugel, 1883; 3rd edn. Paris: Fischbacher, 1897.

Maas, Paul. *Textual Criticism.* Trans. Barbara Flower. Oxford: Clarendon Press, 1958.

Mann, Michael. "Schenker's Contribution to Music Theory." *Music Review* 10 (1949), 3–26.

Marx, A. B. *Die Lehre von der musikalischen Komposition, praktisch-theoretisch.* Vol. II. Leipzig: Breitkopf und Härtel, 1838; 5th edn., 1864.

Maus, Fred. "Recent Ideas and Activities of James K. Randall and Benjamin Boretz: A New Social Role for Music." *Perspectives of New Music* 26/2 (Summer, 1988), 214–222.

Mayrhofer, Robert. *Psychologie des Klanges und die daraus hervorgehende theoretisch-praktische Harmonielehre nebst den Grundlagen der klanglichen Ästhetik.* Leipzig: Fritz Schuberth, 1907.

Die organische Harmonielehre. Berlin and Leipzig: Schuster & Loeffler, 1908.

Mocquereau, André, and J. Gajard ed. *Paléographie Musicale.* Solesmes et Tournai, 1889–.

Moos, Paul. *Die Philosophie der Musik von Kant bis Eduard von Hartmann.* 2nd edn. Stuttgart: Deutsche Verlags-Anstalt, 1922.

Müller-Blattau, Joseph. *Grundzüge einer Geschichte der Fuge.* Königsberg: K. Jüterbock, 1923.

Mueller-Vollmer, Kurt, ed. *The Hermeneutics Reader. Texts of the German Tradition from the Enlightenment to the Present.* New York: Continuum, 1985.

Nadel, Siegfried. *Der duale Sinn der Musik, Versuch einer musikalischen Typologie.* Regensburg: Gustav Bosse, 1931.

Narmour, Eugene. *Beyond Schenkerism: The Need for Alternatives in Musical Analysis.* Chicago and London: University of Chicago Press, 1977.

Nattiez, Jean-Jacques. *Fondements d'une sémiologie de la musique.* Paris: Union générale d'éditions (Série "Ésthetique"), 1975.

Music and Discourse: Toward a Semiology of Music. Trans. Carolyn Abbate. Princeton: Princeton University Press, 1990.

Oppel, Reinhard. "Zur Fugentechnik Bachs." *Bach-Jahrbuch* 18 (1921), 9–48.

Pedersen, Holger. *The Discovery of Language; Linguistic Science in the Nineteenth Century.* Trans. John Spargo. Bloomington, Indiana University Press, 1962.

Potter, Pamela Maxine. Trends in German Musicology, 1918–1945: The Effects of Methodological, Ideological, and Institutional Change on the Writing of Music History. Ph.D. Dissertation, Yale University, 1991.

Proctor, Gregory, and Herbert Riggens. "Levels and the Reordering of Chapters in Schenker's *Free Composition*." *Music Theory Spectrum* 10 (1988), 102–126.

Quine, Willard. *Ontological Relativity and Other Essays.* New York: Columbia University Press, 1969.

Randall, James K. "how music goes." *Perspectives of New Music* 14/2, 15/1 (Spring–Summer–Fall–Winter 1976), 424–497.

Révész, Géza. *The Psychology of a Musical Prodigy* [1916]. Trans. unattributed. New York: Harcourt, Brace & Co., 1925.

Riemann, Hugo. *Musikalische Logik: Hauptzüge der physiologischen und psychologischen Begründung unseres Musiksystems.* Leipzig: C. F. Kahnt, 1874.

Musikalische Syntaxis. Grundriss einer harmonischen Satzsbildungslehre. Leipzig: Breitkopf und Härtel, 1877.

Studien zur Geschichte der Notenschrift. Leipzig: Breitkopf und Härtel, 1878.

Musikalische Dynamik und Agogik. Lehrbuch der musikalischen Phrasirung. Hamburg: D. Rahter, 1884

Handbuch der Harmonielehre. Leipzig: Breitkopf und Härtel, 1887; 3rd edn. 1898; 5th edn. Leipzig: Max Hesse, 1913?

Analysis of J. S. Bach's Wohltemperirtes Clavier. Trans. J. Shedlock. London: Augener, 1893.

Geschichte der Musiktheorie im IX.–XIX. Jahrhundert. Leipzig: Max Hesse, 1898; 2nd edn. 1921.

System der musikalischen Rhythmik und Metrik. Leipzig: Breitkopf und Härtel, 1903.

Grosse Kompositionslehre, II. Berlin and Stuttgart: W. Spemann, 1903.

"Ein Kapital vom Rhythmus." *Die Musik* 3/15 (May 1904), 155–162.

Handbuch der Musikgeschichte I/2. Leipzig: Breitkopf und Härtel, 1905.

Handbuch der Musikgeschichte II/1. Leipzig: Breitkopf und Härtel, 1907.

Kleines Handbuch der Musikgeschichte mit Periodisierung nach Stilprinzipien und Formen. Leipzig: Breitkopf und Härtel, 1908.

Grundriss der Musikwissenschaft . Leipzig: Quelle & Meyer, 1908; 4th edn., ed. Johannes Wolf, 1928.

Die byzantinische Notenschrift im 10. bis 15. Jahrhundert. Leipzig: Breitkopf und Härtel, 1909.

"Die Beck–Aubry'sche 'modale Interpretation' der Troubadourmelodien." *Sammelbände der Internationalen Musik-Gesellschaft* (1909–1910): 569–589.

Musikgeschichte in Beispielen; eine Auswahl von 149 Tonsätzen geistlicher und weltlicher Gesänge und Instrumentalkompositionen zur Veranschaulichung der Entwicklung der Musik im 13.–18. Jahrhundert. Leipzig: E. A. Seemann, 1911; 4th edn. Leipzig: Breitkopf und Härtel, 1929.

Neue Beiträge zur Lösung der Probleme der byzantinischen Notenschrift. Leipzig: Breitkopf und Härtel, 1915.

"Ideen zu einer 'Lehre von den Tonvorstellungen.'" *Jahrbuch der Musikbibliothek Peters für 1914/15.* 21/22 (1916; rpt. Vaduz: Kraus, 1965), 1–26. Introduced and trans. Robert Wason and Elizabeth Marvin as "Riemann's 'Ideen zu einer "Lehre von den Tonvorstellungen"' : an Annotated Translation." *Journal of Music Theory* 36 (1992), 69–117.

"Neue Beiträge zu einer 'Lehre von den Tonvorstellungen.'" *Jahrbuch der Musikbibliothek Peters für 1916.* 23. (1917; rpt. Vaduz: Kraus, 1965), 1–21.

"Die Phrasierung im Lichte einer Lehre von den Tonvorstellungen." *Zeitschrift für Musikwissenschaft.* I/1 (October, 1918): 26–39.

Riemann, Ludwig. "Konsonanzgefühl und mathematische Akustik." *Neue Zeitschrift für Musik* 83 (1916), 385–386.

Rothfarb, Lee. *Ernst Kurth: Selected Writings.* Cambridge: Cambridge University Press, 1991.

"Hermeneutics and Energetics: Analytical Alternatives in the Early 1900s." *Journal of Music Theory* 36 (1992), 43–68.

Schenker, Heinrich. *Ein Beitrag zur Ornamentik, als Einführung zu Ph. Em. Bach's Klavierwerken mitumfassend auch die Ornamentik Haydns, Mozarts, Beethovens etc.*Vienna: Universal Edition, 1904; 2nd edn. 1910.Trans. Hedi Siegel as "A Contribution to the Study of Ornamentation." *Music Forum* IV. New York: Columbia University Press, 1976. 11–139.

*Neue musikalische Theorien und Phantasien.*Vol. I: *Harmonielehre.* Stuttgart and Berlin:J. G. Cotta'sche Buchhandlung Nachfolger, 1906. Ed. and annotated Oswald Jonas, trans. Elisabeth Mann Borgese as *Harmony.* Chicago: University of Chicago Press, 1954.Vol. II: *Kontrapunkt,* Part I. Stuttgart and Berlin: J. G. Cotta'sche Buchhandlung Nachfolger, 1910. Ed. and trans. John Rothgeb and Jürgen Thym as *Counterpoint.* New York: Schirmer Books, 1987.Vol. II: *Kontrapunkt,* Part II.Vienna: Universal Edition, 1922. Ed. and trans.John Rothgeb and Jürgen Thym as *Counterpoint.* New York: Schirmer Books, 1987, vol. II. Vol. III: *Der freie Satz.*Vienna: Universal Edition, 1935. Ed. and trans. Ernst Oster. as *Free Composition.* New York and London: Longman, 1979.

*Beethoven:Die letzen fünf Sonaten:kritische Ausgabe mit Einführung und Erläuterung: Sonata A dur Opus 101.*Vienna: Universal Edition, 1920. Ed. Oswald Jonas. Vienna: Universal Edition, 1972.

Das Meisterwerk in der Musik. Munich: Drei Masken Verlag,Jahrbuch I: 1925, Jahrbuch II:1926.I.ed.and trans.William Drabkin as *The Masterwork in Music: A Yearbook.* Cambridge: Cambridge University Press, 1994; II. ed.William Drabkin, trans. Ian Bent, John Rothgeb, William Drabkin, Hedi Siegel. Cambridge: Cambridge University Press, 1996.

Schering, Arnold. "Die Lehre von den musikalischen Figuren." *Kirchenmusikalisches Jahrbuch* 21 (1908), 106–114.

Musikalische Bildung und Erziehung zum musikalischen Hören. Leipzig: Quelle & Meyer, 1911; 4th edn., 1924.

"Kritik:Wilhelm Werker, *Studien über die Symmetrie im Bau der Fugen ...*" *Bach-Jahrbuch* 19 (1922), 72–88.

Das Symbol in der Musik. Leipzig: Koehler und Amelung, 1941.

Schoenberg, Arnold. *Theory of Harmony.*Trans. Roy Carter. Berkeley, University of California Press, 1978.

Schopenhauer, Arthur. *The World as Will and Idea.* Trans. R. B. Haldane and J. Kemp. London: K. Paul, Trench, Trübner & Co, 1896; rpt. New York: AMS Press, 1977.

Spencer, Herbert. "The Origin and Function of Music [1857]." *Essays: Scientific, Political, and Speculative,* vol. I. London: Williams and Norgate, 1868. 210–238.

Steglich, Rudolf. "Das c moll-Präludium aus dem ersten Teil des Wohl-temperierten Klaviers J. S. Bachs." *Bach Jahrbuch* 20 (1923), 1–11.

Stumpf, Karl. *Tonpsychologie.* 2 vols. Leipzig: S. Hirzel, 1883–1900.

"Konsonanz und Konkordanz. Nebst Bemerkungen über Wohlklang und Wolgefälligkeit musikalischer Zusammenklänge." *Beiträge zur Akustik und Musikwissenschaft* 6. Leipzig: J. A. Barth, 1911. 116–150.

"Differenztöne und Konsonanz." *Beiträge zur Akustik und Musikwissenschaft* 6. Leipzig: J. A. Barth, 1911. 151–165.

Die Anfänge der Musik. Leipzig: J. A. Barth, 1911.

Tichenor, Marjorie. "Getting to gnaw all about you." *Perspectives of New Music* 20/1 (Fall–Winter 1981, Spring–Summer 1982), 406–412.

Titchener, Edward. *Lectures on the Experimental Psychology of the Thought-Processes.* New York: Macmillan, 1909. Reprint New York, Arno Press, 1973.

van Hoorn, Willem, and Thom Verhave. "Wilhelm Wundt's Conception of the Multiple Foundations of Scientific Psychology". *Wilhelm Wundt, progressives Erbe, Wissenschaftsentwicklung und Gegenwart: Protokoll des internationalen Symposiums, Leipzig, 1. und 2. November 1979.* Leipzig: Karl-Marx-Universität, 1980. 107–120.

Wagner, Peter. *Einführung in die Gregorianischen Melodien.* Leipzig: Breitkopf und Härtel. I/1911, II/1912, III/1921.

Wallaschek, Richard. *Anfänge der Tonkunst.* Leipzig: J. A. Barth, 1903.

Wellek, Albert. *Musikpsychologie und Musikästhetik; Grundriss der systematischen Musikwissenschaft.* Frankfurt am Main: Akademische Verlagsgesellschaft, 1963.

Typologie der Musikbegabung im deutschen Volke; Grundlegung einer psychologischen Theorie der Musik und Musikgeschichte. Munich: C. H. Beck, 1939.

Werker, Wilhelm. *Studien über die Symmetrie im Bau der Fugen und die motivische Zusammengehörigkeit der Präludien und Fugen des "Wohltemperierten Klaviers" von Johann Sebastian Bach.* Leipzig: Breitkopf und Härtel, 1922.

Westphal, Rudolph. *Allgemeine Theorie der musikalischen Rhythmik seit J. S. Bach auf Grundlage der Antiken und unter Bezugnahme auf ihren historischen Anschluss an die Mittelalterliche.* Leipzig: Breitkopf und Härtel, 1880.

"Die C-Takt-Fugen des Wohltemperierten Claviers." *Musikalisches Wochenblatt* 14 (1883): 237–238, 253–254, 265–267, 278–280, 289–291, 301–303, 313–315, 325–329.

Wiehmayer, Theodor. *Musikalische Rhythmik und Metrik.* Magdeburg: Heinrichshofen, 1917.

Wundt, Wilhelm. *Logik: Einige Untersuchungen der Principien der Erkenntnis und der Methoden wissenschaftlicher Forschung,* vol. III: *Logik der Geisteswissenschaften.* Stuttgart: F. Enke, 1883; 2nd edn., 1908.

Probleme der Völkerpsychologie. Leipzig: E. Wiegandt, 1911.

Yeston, Maury. *The Stratification of Musical Rhythm*. New Haven: Yale University
     Press, 1976.
Zuschneid, Karl. "Das Phrasierungsproblem und die Konkurrenzausgaben von
     Klavierwerken." *Neue Zeitschrift für Musik* 79 (8, 12 August 1912), 451–454,
     478–481.

INDEX OF PROPER NAMES

INDEX OF SUBJECTS